Jane Short   Rachael Roberts
Joanne Gakonga   Andrew Preshous

IELTS Foundation

Study Skills *Second edition*

A self-study course for all Academic Modules

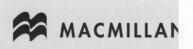

MACMILLAN

Macmillan Education
Between Towns Road, Oxford OX4 3PP
A division of Macmillan Publishers Limited

Companies and representatives throughout the world

ISBN 978-0-230-42578-1

Text, design and illustration © Macmillan Publishers Limited 2012

Written by Jane Short, Rachael Roberts, Joanne Gakonga and Andrew Preshous

This edition published 2012
First published 2004

Designed by eMC Design Ltd.
Illustrated by Stephen Dew and eMC Design Ltd.
Cover photograph by Glow Images/Ingrid Firmhofer/ LOOK-foto

Authors' acknowledgements
The authors would like to thank their families, especially their partners Bill, Chris, Jack and Jo and their children Sam, Kinuthia, Mwathi, Laura and Eleanor for all their support during this project.

Thank you to the many students at Solihull College who trialled material and provided sample answers and valuable feedback.

This book is dedicated to the memory of Wolf Sternagel, a much-loved colleague and friend.

The publishers would like to thank Rosemary Aravanis, Lynn Clark, Paula Clossick, Christine Dowling and Mark Harrison.

The author and publishers would like to thank the following for permission to reproduce their photographs:

Corbis/Darrell Gulin p20, Corbis/Erik Isakson/Tetra Images p60, Corbis/EM Pasieka/SPL p35; Macmillan New Zealand p27.

Graphs and Tables reproduced with the kind permission of: Office for National Statistics pp37 (figs 1,2,3,4), 39 (figs1,2), 40 (fig 7), 41 (fig 8), 43 (fig 11), 44 (fig12), 69.

The authors and publishers are grateful for permission to reprint the following copyright material:

Page 5: IELTS band descriptors reproduced with permission of Cambridge ESOL

Page 20: Extract from 'All of a flutter: Why David Bellamy is getting in a flap over butterflies' by Peter Forbes, copyright © News International Syndication Ltd, first published in *The Times* 01/07/10, pp.26-29. Reprinted by permission of the publisher;

Pages 23–24: Extract from 'Carbon footprint labels: the latest aid for ethical shopping', by Martin Hickman, copyright © The Independent 2010, first published in *The Independent* 13.10.10. Reprinted by permission of the publisher;

Page 27: Shell International for an extract from 'The race is on to create a new world of energy' by Jeroen van der Veer, published in *The Times*, 20/06/2009. Reproduced with permission;

Page 33: Extract from 'Gain or drain? How study abroad affects our economy', by Jessica Moore, copyright © The Independent 2011, first published in *The Independent* 12.05.11. Reprinted by permission of the publisher;

Pages 62–63: University of Texas Press for an extract from "Film in Air: Airspace, In-Flight Entertainment, and Nontheatrical Distribution" by Stephen Groening in *Velvet Light Trap*, Vol 62, pp.4–14, copyright © 2008 by the University of Texas Press. All rights reserved;

Pages 64–65: Extract from 'English language's lost and found: Max Davidson is admitted to Oxford's room of non words' by Max Davidson, copyright © Telegraph Group Limited 2010, first published in *The Daily Telegraph* 17.08.2010. Reprinted by permission of the publisher;

Page 67: Extract from 'Pupils' minds put to work with lessons in meditation' by Sam Lister, copyright © News International Syndication Ltd, first published in *The Times* 12/01/10, p.23. Reprinted by permission of the publisher.

Printed and bound in Thailand
2016 2015 2014 2013 2012
10 9 8 7 6 5 4 3 2 1

Contents

Welcome to *IELTS Foundation Study Skills*. This is a different kind of exam practice book. As well as providing you with exam practice materials, this book will:
- Familiarize you with the different question types you will find in IELTS and give you guided practice in each of them.
- Help you to develop the skills you need to be successful.

There are four parts, corresponding to the four IELTS modules. Each part begins with *skills development*. In these sections you will develop your skills through focused exercises, with detailed guidance given in the key to each question. Next, in the *skills practice* sections, you can put what you have learnt into practice. Finally, the book contains a complete *Practice test*.

As *IELTS Foundation* is aimed at students starting at around 4–5.5, some of the reading and listening texts are shorter or the questions are a little easier than you would find in IELTS, especially towards the beginning. Essential vocabulary is given in a glossary. This will support you as you gradually develop your skills and improve your IELTS score.

For Writing and Speaking both model answers and sample student answers are given, so that you can start to evaluate your own work. Useful language is also provided.

The book is intended to be used for self-study, but could also form the basis of a short intensive IELTS preparation course.

The IELTS Exam

IELTS, or the International English Language Testing System, is an exam designed to assess your level of English, on a scale from 1–9. The score you need will depend upon the course and the university you want to study at, but many students find they need to get an overall band score of 6.

Each section is weighted equally, but it is possible to get half band scores for the Reading and Listening modules (e.g. 5.5, or 6.5), but only whole number bands (e.g. 5, 6, 7, etc) for Speaking and Writing. Overall, therefore, you may get a half band score.

Band 9 – Expert User
Has fully operational command of the language: appropriate, accurate and fluent with complete understanding.

Band 8 – Very Good User
Has fully operational command of the language with only occasional unsystematic inaccuracies and inappropriacies. Misunderstandings may occur in unfamiliar situations. Handles complex detailed argumentation well.

Band 7 – Good User
Has operational command of the language, though with occasional inaccuracies, inappropriacies and misunderstandings in some situations. Generally handles complex language well and understands detailed reasoning.

Band 6 – Competent User
Has generally effective command of the language despite some inaccuracies, inappropriacies and misunderstandings. Can use and understand fairly complex language, particularly in familiar situations.

Band 5 – Modest User
Has partial command of the language, coping with overall meaning in most situations, though is likely to make many mistakes. Should be able to handle basic communication in own field.

Band 4 – Limited User
Basic competence is limited to familiar situations. Has frequent problems in understanding and expression. Is not able to use complex language.

Band 3 – Extremely Limited User
Conveys and understands only general meaning in very familiar situations. Frequent breakdowns in communication can occur.

Band 2 – Intermittent User
No real communication is possible except for the most basic information using isolated words or short formulae in familiar situations and to meet immediate needs. Has great difficulty in understanding spoken and written English.

Band 1 – Non User
Essentially has no ability to use the language beyond possibly a few isolated words.

Band 0 – Did not attempt the test
No assessable information provided.

A summary of each module is outlined below:

Listening

The Listening takes about 40 minutes and each section gets progressively more difficult.

Part	Number of speakers	Number of questions	Situation	Example
1	2	10	social/ general	conversation between a student and a landlord
2	1	10	social/ general	welcoming talk for a group of new students
3	2–4	10	academic	students in a seminar discussion
4	1	10	academic	a university lecture

Question Types: multiple choice, completing notes or sentences, completing or labelling diagrams, charts or tables, classifying, matching and writing short answers.

Exam Tips: You will only hear each section ONCE. However, there is time to look briefly at the questions before each part is played. During the exam, you should write on the question paper, and at the end you will have 10 minutes to transfer answers to the answer sheet. It is important to do this carefully, and check grammar and spelling, as mistakes will lose marks.

Academic Reading

The Reading lasts one hour and there are three reading texts, of increasing difficulty, taken from newspapers, magazines, books and journals. The topics are of general interest, so learners do not have to be experts in the subject area to understand them.

Question Types: multiple choice, choosing *true/false/not given*, or *yes/no/not given*, identifying the view of the writer, completing sentences or notes, completing or labelling diagrams, charts or tables, classifying, matching, choosing paragraph headings and writing short answers. There are 40 questions in total.

Exam Tips: As with the listening module, answers are written on an answer sheet, but no extra time is given for this. It is important that you practise managing your time (20 minutes for each section) so that you can complete the whole module within the hour by reading quickly and efficiently.

Academic Writing

There are two tasks in this module and it lasts 1 hour.

Task	Time	Number of words	Description of task
1	20 minutes	At least 150 words	Describe, compare and contrast information in diagrams, charts or tables, *or* describe the stages of a process, *or* explain how something works.
2	40 minutes	At least 250 words	Give solutions to a problem, *or* present arguments in favour and against an opinion, *or* give and justify an opinion.

Assessment: In order to do well in Task 1, it is important to answer the question clearly, and organize your answer well. This may include grouping data appropriately and describing trends, rather than detailing every piece of information given. Your answer also needs to be accurate and include a good range of vocabulary.

In Task 2, slightly different assessment criteria are used. Here you need to ensure that you answer the question and include a clear and logical argument, giving evidence or examples where appropriate. Your answer also needs to be well organized and have a variety of vocabulary and grammatical structures used accurately.

Exam Tips: It is important to keep to the timings, as Task 2 is longer, and carries slightly more weight than Task 1. It is also important to keep to the word limits, as writing less than the number of words stated is likely to result in a lower score.

Speaking

The Speaking module takes between 11 and 14 minutes and is an oral interview between the learner and an examiner. The interview will be recorded.

Part	Time	Description
1	4–5 minutes	General questions about home, family, studies, etc.
2	3–4 minutes	You are given a card with a topic and 3–4 prompt questions on it. You have 1 minute to prepare, and then have to speak for 1–2 minutes on that topic. At the end, the examiner may ask you a question.
3	4–5 minutes	Further discussion questions relating to the subject in part 2. This section requires you to give opinions, speculate and express reasons.

Assessment: Assessment is based on your fluency, the range, and accuracy of the vocabulary and grammatical structures you use, and your pronunciation.

Exam Tips: Try to relax during the exam, and give more extended responses to questions rather than just 'yes' or 'no' to gain higher marks. You can prepare for this module, for example, by practising speaking for 1–2 minutes on different topics. However, don't memorize long speeches as examiners can usually spot this, and will ask you to talk about something else.

The Listening module is the first part of the IELTS exam. Do this quiz to see how much you know about it.

Quiz

1 How long is the Listening module in total?
   A about 30 minutes   **B** about 40 minutes
   C about 50 minutes
2 How many sections are there?
   A 4   **B** 5   **C** 6
3 How many questions are there in total?
   A 25   **B** 30   **C** 40
4 The first part of the Listening module is the easiest and the last part is the most difficult. True or false?
5 Each section is worth the same number of marks. True or false?
6 There are four situation types in the Listening module. Match the examples with a situation type (A–D). Then number the situation types (A–D) in the order you will hear them.

   • Adam telephones a restaurant to book a table for a party.
   • Professor Jones lectures on climate change.
   • Steve, Mary and Sarah discuss their assignment on water pollution.

   • Mr Green gives a talk on how to open a bank account in the UK.

   ☐ **A** a monologue (one person speaking) in a university situation, e.g. a lecture
   ☐ **B** a monologue relating to social needs, e.g. a speech about arrangements for meals at a conference
   ☐ **C** a dialogue (two people talking together) relating to social needs, e.g. a conversation about travel needs
   ☐ **D** up to four people talking together in an academic situation, e.g. a conversation between a tutor and a student about an assignment

7 How many times do you hear each section?
8 Do you have time to read the questions before you listen?
9 Where should you write your answers?
10 You will lose marks for incorrect spelling. True or false?

Section 1

Remember

• In the dialogues in Section 1 two people are exchanging **factual information** for a **practical** reason.
• Read the instructions carefully so that you know what to do. Underline the key words in the instructions to find out which type of question you need to answer.
• Read the questions carefully and predict what you will hear. Think about **who** is talking, **where** they are and what the **topic** is. In the exam you will only have a short time for this, so do it as quickly as possible.

Skills development

Prediction

Listening module Section 1: Exam information
Number of people: two (a dialogue)
Context: asking for factual information for a social/personal purpose
Example situation: a student applying for a parking permit or someone reporting a stolen bag

1 Read the questions. Think about:
   a who is talking
   b who wants the information
   c where they are
   d what kind of information they want
   e what they want to do with the information

   1 How long has the girl been at the college?
      A a day
      B a few days
      C a couple of weeks

   2 The main building
      A has three floors.
      B is by a lake.
      C has a glass front.

   3 Which door should she take for the accommodation office?
      A the first on the left
      B the second on the right
      C the second on the left

2 ◉01 Listen and answer the questions.

Recognizing repetition and avoiding distracters

1 Read the recording script below. Which information is repeated?

> **Stephan:** ... when you get inside, go straight down the corridor, to the far end, and turn left. You'll see three doors on your left – accommodation is the middle one.
>
> **Keiko:** So, I go along the corridor, turn left, and it's the second door on the left?
>
> **Stephan:** That's right!

2 Look again at question 3. Why might someone choose B?

Completing notes

When completing notes, you will be given a word limit. You can write what you hear, but you might have to change the order of the words or miss some out for the answer to make sense.

e.g.

Students usually look for accommodation conveniently located on campus.

Students prefer accommodation on campus.

1 Rewrite these sentences. Write **NO MORE THAN THREE WORDS** for each answer. Check your answers are grammatically correct.

1 When you choose a university course, think about it carefully. It's a really important decision.

You need to .... before you choose a university course.

2 You might like to study near to your home town, or to go further afield.

You may prefer to go to university .... or in another town or city.

3 The number of students who choose to study overseas is increasing very rapidly.

There has been a rapid rise in the number of students wanting to

....

2 Keiko made some notes about the accommodation available through the college. Read the notes and predict the kind of information you need to listen for.

3 ⊙02 Listen and complete Keiko's notes. Write **NO MORE THAN THREE WORDS** for each answer.

4 Check your answers on page 71.

Three types of accommodation available:

- *Home stay*

  Cost of home stay: (1) _____ per week with meals

- *(2) _____*

- *Private lets*

  College makes sure flats are (3) _____

First name: Keiko

Surname: (4) ....

Nationality: (5) ....

Address: The Sunrise Guest House

(6) ....

Phone number: (7) ....

email address: keiko@hotmail.com

5 ⊙**03** Listen to the final part of the conversation between Keiko and the Accommodation Officer and complete the form.

Remember
All answers must be spelt and punctuated correctly.

Remember
- Names of people and places always begin with capital letters. You will lose marks if you don't include them.
- When you listen for numbers that sound similar (e.g. 15 and 50) listen carefully for the stressed syllable (e.g. *fif'teen* or *'fifty*) to help you tell the difference.

Listening for numbers and letters

1 ⊙**04** How do you say these numbers in English? Listen and check your answers.

15   50   162   £3.25   47%   0.54   12,651

2 ⊙**05** How do you say these letters in English? Listen and check your answers.

U   Y   J   O   G   X   I   P
Z   W   H   A   Q   R   E   B

3 ⊙**06** How do you say these punctuation marks in English? Listen and check your answers.

1 /
2 -
3 :
4 ;
5 . (in web addresses)

4 ⊙**07** Listen and complete the notes with the appropriate words or numbers.

1 The man's name is ....
2 The answer is ....
3 The address is ....
4 Everest is .... high.
5 His name is ....
6 The address is ....
7 Her test score was ....
8 His favourite author is ....
9 The phone number is ....
10 The reference number is ....
11 The woman's name is ....
12 The address is ....
13 The web address is ....
14 The man wants to make an appointment with ....
15 The registration number is ....

Skills practice

Now practise the skills you have learnt by listening to the recording and answering questions **1** and **2**.

Questions 1–2

⊙ 08 For questions 1 and 2, listen and choose the correct answer.

1 How many people can the restaurant seat in one group?
  A 10
  B 8
  C 18
  D 24

2 How many people will be able to sit at each table?
  A 10
  B 8
  C 15
  D 16

Questions 3–5

While he was on the phone, Dan made some notes. For questions **3–5**, listen and complete the notes. Write **NO MORE THAN THREE WORDS** for each answer.

For parties, the restaurant usually serves a (3) .... for a fixed price. There are three choices for each course, for example for starters there is prawn cocktail, soup or antipasto. At least one of the choices is (4).. Also included in the price is (5) ....

Questions 6–9

For questions **6–9**, listen and complete the booking form.

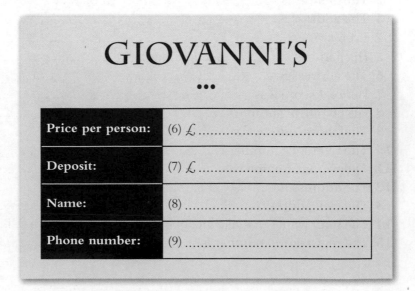

GIOVANNI'S	
•••	
Price per person:	(6) £ ....
Deposit:	(7) £ ....
Name:	(8) ....
Phone number:	(9) ....

The listening passages in Section 2 focus on exchanging factual information for practical purposes. The passages may be dialogues or short talks given by one person (monologues) about **how to do something**. When you start listening ask yourself what the situation is and what the listener can do when they have the information.

Skills development

> **Listening module Section 2: Exam information**
> Number of people: one (a monologue)
> Context: non-academic, social needs
> Example situation: an informal talk on how to open a bank account

Using key words for prediction

1 Read questions **1–3** below and <u>underline</u> the important words. Can you think of synonyms for these words?

Remember
- The order of the questions follows the recording, so you can answer them in order.
- Think of synonyms or other ways of saying the important words.
- In a multiple-choice question you may have to choose two or more answers.

2 ⊙09 Now listen and answer questions **1–3**.

    1 The programme
      A gives information about used car sales.
      B tells you the best way to buy a car.
      C tells you the most popular way to sell a car.
      D looks at different ways of buying a new car.

    2 Which of the following reasons does the presenter give for someone wanting to buy a used car? Circle **TWO** letters **A–D**.
      A You are a new driver.
      B You have had an accident in your old car.
      C Your car is too old to be repaired.
      D You are not in a hurry to drive.

    3 One advantage of a dealer is
      A they have a lot of room to show you the cars.
      B they are cheap.
      C you have a legal right to return the car if something goes wrong.
      D they are honest.

Eliminating wrong answers

If you can eliminate even one or two wrong answers, you will improve your chances of getting the right answer.

3 ⊙09 Listen again and decide why the other answers to questions **1–3** above are wrong.

Completing a summary

Remember
Contractions such as *he's* count as two words.

1 Read this summary. For each gap, predict:
- the type of word missing (e.g. noun/verb/adjective)
- the kind of information it is asking for (use the context to help you)

A (1) .... way to buy a car is privately. Usually this is done by looking through the (2) .... and contacting the person selling the car directly. The (3) .... is that you will not get a warranty. If you are not knowledgeable about cars, you should have the car checked (4) ....

You could also buy a car at auction. This could be very risky as you won't have (5) .... to inspect it properly before you buy it.

2 ⊙10 Listen and complete the summary.

Skills practice

Questions 1–4

🔘⓫ Read through questions **1–4**. Use the skills you have just practised and then listen to the recording and write the correct letter **A**, **B** or **C** next to questions **1–4**. You can choose any letter more than once.

What does Jenny Arnold tell the students about preparing for holidays abroad?

A They might ...
B They should ...
C They should not ...

1 find out about necessary vaccinations.
2 find out just before they leave.
3 have to pay for vaccinations.
4 have to pay for malaria tablets.

Questions 5–6

Read through questions **5–6** and complete the summary. Write **NO MORE THAN THREE WORDS** for each answer.

It is important to buy some (5) .... before you leave, even though it may be (6) ...., especially if you plan to do adventure sports. It will make your holiday more relaxing if you know that you could always get home safely.

Questions 7–9

Read through questions **7–9** and then complete the sentences. Write **NO MORE THAN THREE WORDS** for each answer.

- While you are away, you should be careful of getting burnt by (7) .... at midday.

- You should be careful of drinking local water and using it when you (8) ....

- If you get an upset stomach, drink plenty of (9) ....

Skills development

Listening for specific speakers

> **Listening module Section 3: Exam information**
> Number of people: up to four people
> Context: education or training
> Example situations: a tutor and a student discussing an assignment, or a seminar situation with several students talking

🔊 **12** Listen and answer the questions.

1 How many speakers are there in the conversation? How do you know?
2 What are their names?
3 How many times does each person speak?

Listening for specific information/short answers

1 Read the questions below and <u>underline</u> the key words. Which answer is a number? Which is a location or a situation? What *recent ecological problems* can you think of?

2 🔊 **13** Listen and answer the questions. Write **NO MORE THAN THREE WORDS OR A NUMBER** for each answer.

1 Which **TWO** kinds of recent ecological problems does Anand mention?
   A ....
   B ....

2 What is the word limit for the assignment?
   ....

3 Where did Robert get his idea for a topic from?
   ....

Completing a table

1 Look at the table. Which questions ask you to identify types of pollution? Which answer is a date?

2 🔊 **14** Listen and complete the table. Write **NO MORE THAN THREE WORDS** for each answer.

Pollution problem	Solution provided by	Completed
(1)...........................	City Council	(2).............................
Boat traffic	(3)............................	next year
(4)...........................	(5)...........................	ongoing project

Matching

For matching tasks, you have to match statements in a list to one of three options. The options may be categories, situations or conditions. There may be more than one statement for each option.

Remember
You may have to use the options more than once.

1 Look at the question below and <u>underline</u> the key words.

2 ⊙15 For questions **1–4**:
How do each of the following relate to the problem of pollution in the harbour?

   1 local diving clubs
   2 marine life
   3 bad weather
   4 jet skis and small motor boats

   A benefit from the problem
   B cause the problem
   C solve the problem

Spelling

As in Section 2, sometimes words are spelt out for you, but often they are not. Even if the words are not spelt out, you must still spell them correctly.

1 ⊙16 Listen and complete the sentences.

   1 The college is on the .... of an old castle.
   2 The meeting will be held on ....
   3 Please hand your essays in by next ....
   4 We .... that you take the test in May.
   5 The course is .... and highly beneficial.
   6 .... rose dramatically in 2001.
   7 I would .... you to do your homework.
   8 He was a very successful ....
   9 Different .... have different management systems.
   10 The maths exam was .... than the statistics test.
   11 Studying abroad can help you become more ....
   12 .... unwanted emails, or spam, is a growing problem.

2 Now check your answers on page 73.

3 Here is a list of words common in academic writing. Which **THREE** are spelt wrongly? Use your dictionary to check form and meaning.

accompany	consent	evident	percieved	suficient	specified

Skills practice

Questions 1–4

🔘**17** Use the skills you have just practised to listen to the recording and complete the table. Write **NO MORE THAN THREE WORDS OR A NUMBER** for each answer.

	'A' Levels	Foundation Course
Length of course	2 years	1 year
Number of subjects studied	2–3	(1)............................
English language support given	often none	(2).................... per ....
Main type of assessment	exam(s)	(3)............................
Most popular with	(4)............................	overseas students

Questions 5–8

Write **NO MORE THAN THREE WORDS OR A NUMBER** for each answer.

5 What kind of English does Cathy study? ....

6 What does she say is different from her language? ....

7 Cathy studies the following modules:
- economic theory
- marketing strategies
- ....

8 What does Brenda think about Cathy's course? ....

Questions 9–12

For questions **9–12**:

if they refer to Millford University write **M**

       Ainsley University write **A**

       Parmouth University write **P**

 9 Which university has given Cathy a conditional offer? ....

10 Which university usually requires an IELTS score of 6.5? ....

11 Which university has a good reputation for Business Studies? ....

12 Which university is in a good location? ....

Skills development

Labelling a diagram with numbered parts

Listening module Section 4: Exam information
Number of people: one (a monologue)
Context: education or training
Example situation: a lecture. The subject may be quite specific, but remember that you do not need any specialist knowledge to answer the questions.

1 Look at the following three diagrams.

   1 Which one shows a plan or map?
   2 Which one shows a process?
   3 Which one shows an object?

Diagram 1

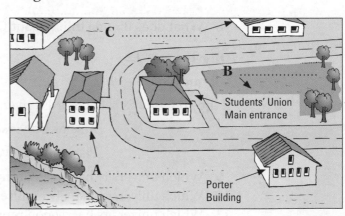

Object

A ....

B ....

Diverging rays

Concave lens

Diagram 2

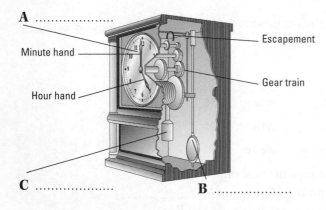

A ....

Minute hand

Hour hand

C ....

Escapement

Gear train

B ....

Diagram 3

C ....

B ....

Students' Union
Main entrance

A ....

Porter
Building

2 🔘18 Now listen and complete the labels on the diagrams.

3 Look at diagram 4. What does it show? Describe the positions of the numbered parts.

Remember
Study the diagram. Note what it shows and what positions things are in.

4 🔘19 Listen and complete the labels. Write **NO MORE THAN THREE WORDS** for each answer.

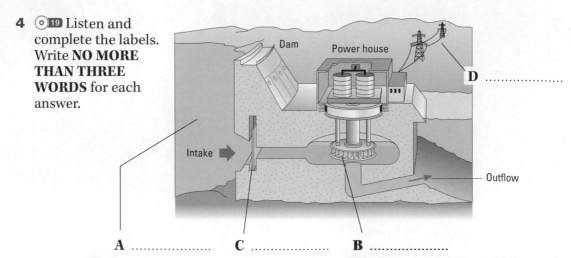

Dam

Power house

D ....

Intake

Outflow

A ....

C ....

B ....

Labelling a flow chart

1 Look at the flow chart below. Which answer is a number?

2 ⊙20 Complete the flow chart. Write **NO MORE THAN THREE WORDS OR A NUMBER** for each answer.

GENERATOR	☐ Create power
TRANSMISSION SUBSTATION Power at 1 .... volts	☐ Transforms electricity to high voltages
LOCAL POWER SUBSTATION Power at 7,200 volts	☐ Reduces voltage ☐ 2 .... ☐ Can turn off power if necessary
TRANSFORMER BOX/DRUM Power at 240 volts	☐ Lowers power to make it suitable for 3 .... service
CIRCUIT BREAKER/FUSE	☐ Safety device to minimize 4 ....

Sentence completion

1 Is the information you need in the sentences below a noun, a verb or an adjective?

    1 Two positive aspects of hydroelectricity are that it is .... and ....

    2 One limiting factor of hydroelectricity is that it requires ....

2 ⊙21 Listen and answer the questions.

Listening for signpost words

Signpost words are words or phrases that tell a listener what the speaker is going to talk about next, e.g. *Right,* or *Anyway* indicate a change of subject and *for instance* indicates when the speaker is going to give an example.

Look at these extracts from the lecture on hydroelectricity. What do the underlined words indicate?

1 <u>I want to move on</u> today <u>to</u> a form of power that many would argue is far superior.
    A contrasting information
    B introducing a new topic
    C summing up

2 Right, <u>as you can see</u>, under the dam there is a control gate ...
    A introducing a new topic
    B drawing attention to a visual
    C emphasizing a point

3 <u>As we've said</u>, the power leaves the generator and enters ...
    A recapping or reviewing information
    B summing up
    C adding extra information

Remember
- You may be able to use words from the text, or you may need to change the form of the words, e.g. *reliable flow of water* (= four words), change to *reliable water flow* (= three words).
- You don't always need to include articles.

Remember

- You will have 10 minutes to transfer your answers to the answer sheet at the end of the exam.
- Write your name and your candidate number on the answer sheet.
- You have to complete the answer sheet in pencil.
- Take great care that you transfer your answers correctly – if you have the right answer in the wrong place on the answer sheet you will not get any marks. Use a ruler to help you if necessary.
- Check that your spelling is correct.
- You will not lose marks for an incorrect answer, so don't leave any blank spaces.

Skills practice

Questions 1–4

⊙22 Now practise the skills you have learnt by listening to the recording and completing the sentences below. Write **NO MORE THAN THREE WORDS OR A NUMBER** for each answer.

1 Oil formation began between 10 million and .... years ago.
2 Dead plankton sank to the sea bed to mix with the ....
3 Layers of sediment put pressure and .... on the source rock.
4 Oil collects in porous rock, e.g. ....

Questions 5–7

Complete the diagram below. Write **NO MORE THAN THREE WORDS** for each answer.

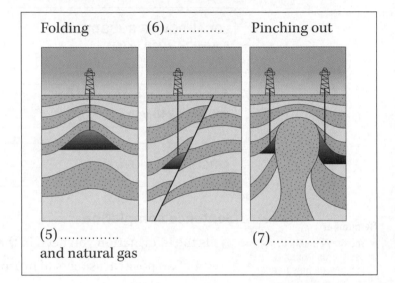

Folding   (6) ....   Pinching out

(5) ....
and natural gas

(7) ....

Questions 8–12

Complete the flow chart using **NO MORE THAN THREE WORDS** for each answer.

Initial stages	Preparation for drilling	Drilling
Legal issues are settled.	Land is cleared and levelled. (8) .... may be built. A well is dug or a source of local (9) .... is found. Large, plastic-lined hole called a (10) .... is made. A cellar is dug at the site of (11)	Main hole begun with smaller drill. (12) Main rig is ....

Now go back to the quiz on page 7 and fill in the answers that you did not manage to do before.

Study Skills: Reading

How much do you know about the IELTS Academic Reading module? Do the quiz below to find out.

Quiz

1 How long is the Academic Reading module?
   A 90 minutes   **B** 60 minutes
   C 11–14 minutes

2 How many reading passages are there?
   A one   **B** four   **C** three

3 How many questions are there in total?
   A 35   **B** 40   **C** 55

4 Where can the reading passages come from? Tick any that you think are true.
   A magazines ☐
   B newspapers ☐
   C journals ☐
   D letters ☐
   E books ☐
   F advertisements ☐

5 There is extra time for transferring your answers to the answer sheet at the end of the exam.
   True or false?

6 Texts and tasks are easier at the beginning of the exam than at the end.
   True or false?

7 All the questions are multiple choice.
   True or false?

8 At least one text contains detailed, logical argument.
   True or false?

In this section you will be looking at the skills you need to do well in the IELTS Academic Reading module and practising different question types.

Reading Passages 1 and 2

Skills development

Skimming for gist

Look quickly over the whole text to get an idea of what it is about. This will help when you come to look at the text in more detail, and is worth doing even when under pressure of time in the exam.

Read Reading Passage 1 in no more than three minutes and decide on the best general heading.

Remember
- Read the first sentence of each paragraph. This is usually the topic sentence, or the sentence that introduces the main topic of the paragraph.
- Don't worry if you don't know all the vocabulary. It may not be necessary in order to answer the questions.

List of headings
  i Beautiful butterflies
 ii The life cycle of the butterfly
iii Butterflies in decline
 iv Butterflies and farming

A Butterflies vie with bees as humanity's favourite insects. The bees have it in terms of economic importance, and the current threats to bee colonies are bringing home how much we all depend on them for the pollination of our crops. And aren't bees and butterflies opposites: the bees all industry and discipline and usefulness; the butterflies a byword for 'airiness and frivolity', as the great 19th century explorer and naturalist Henry Walter Bates put it?

B Certainly butterflies are loved partly for their extravagant beauty and the decoration they bring to summer days. Their abstract wing patterns were clearly Modern Art before humans had got round to inventing it.

C But Henry Walter Bates followed his remark about the frivolity of butterflies with this: 'The study of butterflies … instead of being despised, will someday be valued as one of the most important branches of Biological science.' That day is coming to pass.

D In natural ecosystems there are some organisms that are more sensitive to change than others: they are the canaries in the coalmine, harbingers. Lichens are often cited as early warning indicators of pollution, but although rather gorgeous in their way, if they disappeared their absence would not be felt as keenly as that of the butterflies.

E Butterflies are ecologically vulnerable because they are specialists. Everyone knows that they love colourful, scented flowers rich in nectar, but in their larval phase – the caterpillars – they have stringent requirements for quite different plants. Most caterpillars feed on a very limited range of plants, many on a single species, and it is almost never one of the plants on which the adults feed. Some adult butterflies, in fact, don't feed at all: their sole purpose is to mate and lay eggs. For some species this takes a few days only, and they rely on the energy stores that they are born with (fruit of the caterpillar's munching). Professor David Bellamy, passionate naturalist and conservationist, laments the loss of the butterfly paradise he experienced as a boy growing up during the Second World War, when every bomb site quickly filled with flowers. But butterfly-luring flowers. But it's the bombshell of modern agribusiness, with its monocultures, herbicides and pesticides and hence loss of biodiversity, that he blames for the dramatic declines in many of our native butterflies.

F But he reminds us that hard economics and wild nature are not irrevocably at odds. 'We can have our cake and eat it. Because without bees and butterflies what would pollinate our plants?' He paints a vivid picture of the rise and fall of the butterfly-friendly environment in Britain. 'Ten thousand years ago woolly mammoths roamed here in Ice Age conditions. Seven thousand years ago, as the climate warmed, England was mostly forest, and there would have been few butterflies in such dense woodland. It was Neolithic farmers and their successors who created the patchwork of fields, hedges and copses – a landscape in which butterflies could thrive.'

G For Bellamy, it is this stewardship of the environment that matters. Having created, through traditional agriculture, a landscape that both fed us and fostered biodiversity, we need to return to good husbandry: 'gamekeepers are our best guardians', he says. Bellamy is passionate about reinstating a butterfly-friendly habitat – 'As we made it, we can mend it. It will come back quickly' – and he looks forward to 'the renaissance of the British landscape', quoting Churchill: 'a landscape worth dying for'.

Glossary
Pollination – to place pollen from one flower on another flower in order to help it to produce seed
Frivolity – silly behaviour or attitudes
Harbingers – signs that something will happen soon, often something bad
Lichens – a small soft plant that grows on surfaces such as trees and walls
Larval – the form that butterflies take after they have left the egg and before they develop into their adult form
Mammoths – animals similar to elephants with long hair that lived a very long time ago
Stewardship – the way in which someone organizes and looks after something (e.g. land)
Renaissance – new interest in something that makes it popular again

Matching headings to paragraphs

This is a common IELTS task. It will help you understand how the text is organized and can help you identify where to find the information you need to answer the questions about the text.

Reading Passage 1 has seven paragraphs **A–G**. Choose the most suitable heading for paragraphs **B–G** from the list of headings below.

List of headings

   i The life cycle of a caterpillar
  ii Butterflies' susceptibility to changes in nature E
 iii Our responsibility to care for the environment F G
  iv Contamination and living creatures D
   v A countryside suitable for butterflies E
  vi Modern Art
 vii Research into butterflies C
viii Contrasting bees and butterflies
  ix The beauty of butterflies B

Labelling diagrams

Label the chart below using words from the box and information from paragraphs **E** and **F**.

> **A** forests   **B** Ice Age   **C** agribusiness   **D** Neolithic farming

The rise and fall of the butterfly population

1. B — ICE AGE / ICE
2. A — Forest
3. D — Neolithic farming
4. C — agribusiness

Multiple choice

1 Butterflies are important because
   A they are attractive.
   B some adults do not feed at all.
   C they give early warning of ecological damage.
   D they migrate every year.

2 Pollution affects butterflies in particular because
   A they have a very selective diet.
   B they rely on stored energy to survive.
   C they pollinate the plants.
   D they're attracted to lichen.

3 The cause of the decline of the butterfly population is
   A the Second World War.
   B the use of chemicals on the crops.
   C biodiversity.
   D traditional agriculture.

This type of multiple choice question asks you to choose two answers from a group of five or three answers from a group of seven.

4 Circle **TWO** letters **A–E**.

   Butterflies were plentiful when
   A England was covered in ice.
   B there was a lot of woodland.
   C farmland was first developed.
   D farmers started using pesticides.
   E there was a lot of wasteland.

5 Circle **THREE** letters **A–G**.

   Caterpillars and butterflies usually eat
   A only once a day.
   B a wide variety of plants.
   C nothing.
   D different plants from each other.
   E only one type of plant.
   F nectar from highly perfumed flowers.
   G a small selection of plants.

Guessing meaning from context

1 Look at paragraph **E** again. Notice how the writer avoids repetition by using synonyms or related words.

specialists	*have stringent requirements*
larval phase	*caterpillars*
feed	*munching*
monoculture	*loss of biodiversity*

E Butterflies are ecologically vulnerable because they are specialists. Everyone knows that they love colourful, scented flowers rich in nectar, but in their larval phase – the caterpillars – they have stringent requirements for quite different plants. Most caterpillars feed on a very limited range of plants, many on a single species, and it is almost never one of the plants on which the adults feed. Some adult butterflies, in fact, don't feed at all: their sole purpose is to mate and lay eggs. For some species this takes a few days only, and they rely on the energy stores that they are born with (fruit of the caterpillar's munching). Professor David Bellamy, passionate naturalist and conservationist, laments the loss of the butterfly paradise he experienced as a boy growing up during the Second World War, when every bomb site quickly filled with flowers. But butterfly-luring flowers. But it's the bombshell of modern agribusiness, with its monocultures, herbicides and pesticides and hence loss of biodiversity, that he blames for the dramatic declines in many of our native butterflies.

> **1** What kind of butterflies have declined? What part of speech is this word? What other part of speech can it be?
> **2** What part of speech is *butterfly-luring*?

2 Look at paragraph **G** again. Find more words in the paragraph with a similar meaning to those circled.

Remember
If you think you have guessed the meaning of a word correctly, try replacing the word in the passage with another word with this meaning. Does it make sense?

> **G** For Bellamy, it is this stewardship of the environment that matters. Having created through traditional agriculture, a landscape that both fed us and fostered biodiversity, we need to return to good husbandry: 'gamekeepers are our best guardians', he says. Bellamy is passionate about reinstating a butterfly-friendly habitat – 'As we made it, we can mend it. It will come back quickly' – and he looks forward to 'the renaissance of the British landscape', quoting Churchill: 'a landscape worth dying for'.

Skills practice

Now practise the skills you have learnt by answering the questions on Reading Passage 2.

Reading Passage 2

A Shoppers familiar with seeing fair trade, organic or rainforest labels during their weekly shop will have to get used to another logo: the carbon footprint. Leading food brands are increasingly using the Government's black footprint logo and, according to research published today, it will become the second most common ethical label in UK shops by the end of this year.

B The Centre for Retail Research forecasts that annual sales of the Carbon Reduction Label run by the publicly funded Carbon Trust would hit £2 billion by the end of 2010, putting it behind only the Red Tractor farm assurance scheme (£10 billion), but ahead of the Soil Association's organic mark (£1.5 billion); Fairtrade (£800 million); RSPCA Freedom Foods (£800 million), and the smaller Rainforest Alliance and Marine Stewardship Council schemes.

C For shoppers, the black footprint logo shows that producers are working behind the scenes with the Carbon Trust to identify and reduce carbon emissions that cause global warming. In some cases, the labels also display the amount of CO_2 generated by each product, giving consumers a greater insight into how much unseen pollution is caused by their purchases – sometimes with surprising results. The amount of CO_2 emitted generally weighs more than the product, and there can be substantial variations between different brands or types of the same product.

D Tesco has been the most enthusiastic supporter of the scheme, carrying out a commitment made three years ago to carbon label all of its 70,000 food lines. It has so far put footprints on 100 own-brand products, including semi-skimmed milk (800 grams per pint); orange juice (1.1 kg per litre); and toilet roll (1.1 grams per sheet). Walkers, the UK's best-selling crisps, and baker Kingsmill, which is owned by Primark's parent company Associated British Foods, have adopted the idea too. Shoppers can already see that at 1.3 kg of CO_2 per 800 grams, a loaf of wholemeal bread generates 15 times more carbon dioxide than a small packet of crisps (80 grams).

E However, other products have not been included, possibly because shoppers would be put off by how much pollution they generate. Meat has 'astronomical' emissions according to one supermarket source, something borne out by research. A study by Japan's National Institute of Livestock and Grassland Science found three years ago that 1 kg of beef released the equivalent of 36 kg of CO_2. Alcohol, too, has high emissions. While a 330 ml can of Coca-Cola® has 170 grams, Adnams eco-bitter East Green has 432 grams per half-litre. Consumers can, however, slash the impact of their purchases by using the same products differently – washing clothes at 30°C rather than 40°C saves 160 grams of CO_2.

F Currently, these insights are interesting, but they could become more important. Two years ago the Commons Environmental Audit committee said the Government should give everyone a personal carbon allowance. Euan Murray, the Carbon Trust's head of footprinting, said he did not know if all products would eventually be carbon labelled, but added: 'We are increasingly seeing people recognise that things have a carbon footprint, and they want to do something about it.'

Glossary
Carbon footprint – a calculation of the amount of carbon dioxide (CO_2) that an activity uses (e.g. producing food, driving a car, watching television)

Question 1

Choose the most appropriate heading for Reading Passage 2 from the list below.

List of headings
  i Carbon reduction
 ii Ethical labels
iii Carbon footprint labelling

Questions 2–4

Reading Passage 2 has six paragraphs **A–F**. Choose the most appropriate headings for paragraphs **B**, **C** and **D** from the list below.

  2 Paragraph B ....
  3 Paragraph C ....
  4 Paragraph D ....

List of headings
   i Controlling your carbon footprint
  ii The carbon footprint of household products
 iii Reducing carbon emissions
  iv The future of carbon footprinting
   v The carbon footprint of meat
  vi Ethical labels
 vii Personal carbon quotas

Questions 5–8

Complete the table below. Choose **NO MORE THAN THREE WORDS OR A NUMBER** from Reading Passage 2 for each answer.

Product	Weight	CO_2 emission
(5)	1 litre	1.1 kg
(6)	800 grams	1.3 kg
(7)	(8)	36 kg

Questions 9–11

Which **THREE** purposes of the black footprint logo does the author mention?

9 Purpose 1
  A to inform consumers about the amount of CO_2 generated for each product
  B to prevent customers from buying high CO_2 products
  C to make sure animals are fairly treated during the production of meat
  D to encourage customers to buy their own brand

10 Purpose 2
  A to protect marine animals
  B to reduce the sale of alcohol in supermarkets
  C to show that manufacturers are trying to reduce CO_2 pollution worldwide
  D to encourage customers to eat more healthily

11 Purpose 3
  A to promote vegetarianism
  B to limit customers' choice of products
  C to encourage customers to buy products from developing countries
  D to help consumers contribute to the reduction of CO_2 emissions

Questions 12–14

Label the chart. Choose your answers from the box.

meat   milk   Coca-Cola®   toilet roll   crisps   hot water   beer

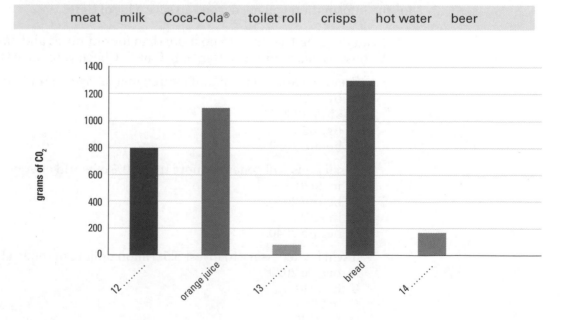

Questions 15–17

Choose the correct letter, **A**, **B**, **C** or **D**.

15 The biggest ethical label is
    A the Soil Association.
    B RSPCA Freedom Foods.
    C the Red Tractor.
    D Fairtrade.

16 Some products still do not have carbon footprint labels because
    A they are impossible to calculate.
    B the figures are very high.
    C they are insignificant.
    D they vary across brands.

17 The Government has recommended that
    A consumers should wash their clothes at 30°C.
    B every product should have a carbon label.
    C everybody should have a limited CO_2 allowance.
    D high carbon rated products should be restricted.

Skills development

Skimming for gist

Skim the text and choose the sentence from **A–C** that best summarizes the main message of the passage.

  A In the future biofuels will replace fossil fuels.
  B Cleaner fossil fuels will reduce CO_2 production.
  C In the future energy will be supplied by a wide range of fuels.

Scanning to find information quickly

It is important to have an overall understanding of the text but you do not always have to read all parts of the text in the same detail. If you can quickly identify where to look for the information you need, you can save a lot of time.

1 Read Reading Passage 3 in no more than four minutes and answer the questions. Choose the appropriate letter, A, B, C or D. Check your answers on page 75.

    1 Fuel cell cars will be manufactured in increasing numbers
        A by 2020.
        B after 2030.
        C by 2050.
        D before 2020.

    2 Fossil fuels will generate more than 50% of world energy
        A in 2020.
        B before 2030.
        C in 2050.
        D before 2040.

    3 It will be necessary to invest 5.5 trillion dollars in renewable energy
        A before 2020.
        B in 2040.
        C in 2050.
        D by 2030.

ALTERNATIVE FUELS

A We stand at the early dawn of a new energy future. It will be powered by alternative energy and cleaner fossil fuels. If governments adopt the right rules and incentives, by the middle of this century renewable sources will provide nearly 30 per cent of the world's energy. Society will be on the road toward sustainable mobility. The world's highways will rumble and whir with vehicles powered by all manner of energy: petrol, diesel (yes, still there), electricity, biofuels, natural gas and hydrogen.

B In the years ahead, conventional diesel and petrol cars will go further on every litre of fuel. Biofuels will account for up to 10 per cent of liquid transport fuel in the next few decades. Planners at Shell, one of the world's largest energy and petrochemical companies, think that by 2020 up to 15 per cent of new cars worldwide could be hybrid electrics, such as Toyota's Prius, some of them capable of plugging in to recharge their batteries. After 2030, fuel cell vehicles powered by hydrogen will be a small but growing part of the fleet. By 2050, more than a billion extra vehicles are expected on the world's roads, more than double today's total.

C Greater variety of fuel choices will be a boon for consumers. Different fuels will be stronger in different regions. In South America, biofuels will likely predominate. In Brazil, ethanol from sugar cane already supplies more than 40 per cent of demand for petrol. China, meanwhile, plans to expand production and use of hybrid and electric vehicles, tapping its vast coal deposits to generate power.

D As more vehicles go electric, the environmental footprint of the world's power generators will become even more important. Wind, solar and hydropower will account for 30 per cent of electricity generation by 2030, up from about 18 per cent today. Many new coal-fired power plants are expected to capture CO_2 emissions and store it safely underground, rather than pump it into the atmosphere. Plants increasingly will turn coal into a gas, rather than burn it. They will then burn the gas to generate power, or use it as raw material for a variety of chemical products, while CO_2 will be captured and stored. Such integrated plants will begin to resemble refineries. Likewise, refineries can 'gasify' heavy oils – and use the gas to produce hydrogen – and generate heat and electricity – while capturing and storing the CO_2.

E Indeed, fossil fuels; coal, oil and natural gas, will continue to provide more than half the world's energy in 2050, building a long bridge to an era when alternatives can take over. A growing population and higher standards of living for billions of people in the developing world will mean that we need all available sources of energy to keep the world's economies humming. So, while the world races to build up alternative fuels, it must also find new sources of fossil fuels, including unconventional ones, such as oil sands. And we must accelerate efforts to make fossil fuels cleaner, by reducing the CO_2 emitted in their production and use.

F None of this will be easy, or cheap. Industry and government regulations must change on a huge scale and at an unprecedented pace. According to the International Energy Agency, by 2030 we will need to invest $5.5 trillion merely in renewable energy. That's like buying more than 18,000 Boeing 747 jumbo jets at $300 million apiece (only about 14,000 have been built since its introduction in 1970). Billions more must go into upgrading electricity transmission networks to handle increased demand and the on-and-off power generated by wind and solar.

G Much of this money will come from private companies, but governments will need to continue using tax credits and other incentives to encourage the growth of renewables. They are still small relative to the world's overall energy needs. Including hydropower, renewables account for about seven per cent of global energy. Wind today supplies about one per cent, with approximately 70,000 turbines. Biofuels, thanks partly to billions of dollars in government subsidies, now also supply about one per cent.

Glossary

Fossil fuels – fuels such as coal or oil, made from decayed material from plants or animals that lived many thousands of years ago
Incentive – something that makes you want to do something because you know that you will benefit by doing this
Sustainable – using methods that do not harm the environment
Biofuels – fuel that is made from living things or from something their bodies produce
Hybrid – a mixture of two things or styles
Boon – something useful that brings great benefits or makes your life easier
Ethanol – a chemical which comes from processing sugar and the type of alcohol in alcoholic drinks
Hydropower – power from water in rivers, the sea and artificial dams
Gasify – to convert fossil fuel, such as coal, into gas

2 Read questions **1–3**. Before you answer them, decide in which paragraph **A–G** you will find the answer. Look at the summarizing sentences in exercise 1 to help you.

　1 How will future coal-fired power plants prevent captured CO_2 from reaching the atmosphere?
　2 How can we make better use of fossil fuels in the future?
　3 How will increased demand for electricity be met in the future?

3 Scan the text again to check you have chosen the correct paragraph.

Short answer questions

Look at extracts **i–iii** from Reading Passage 3 and answer questions **1–3**. Underline any words that will answer each question.

　1 How will future coal-fired power plants prevent captured CO_2 from reaching the atmosphere?
　2 How can we make better use of fossil fuels in the future?
　3 How will increased demand for electricity be met in the future?

　i Many new coal-fired power plants are expected to capture CO_2 emissions and store it safely underground, rather than pump it into the atmosphere. Plants increasingly will turn coal into a gas, rather than burn it. They will then burn the gas to generate power, or use it as raw material for a variety of chemical products, while CO_2 will be captured and stored.
　ii So, while the world races to build up alternative fuels, it must also find new sources of fossil fuels, including unconventional ones, such as oil sands. And we must accelerate efforts to make fossil fuels cleaner, by reducing the CO_2 emitted in their production and use.
　iii Billions more must go into upgrading electricity transmission networks to handle increased demand and the on-and-off power generated by wind and solar means.

Remember

The instructions will tell you how many words you should use, e.g. '**NO MORE THAN THREE WORDS AND/ OR A NUMBER** from the passage', '**ONE WORD ONLY**' or '**NO MORE THAN TWO WORDS**'. You will lose marks if you write more than the number of words you are asked to use.

Remember

• You do not necessarily need to include articles in your three words e.g. (*the*) *on-and-off power*.

• Look out for referring expressions like *the former*, *the latter*, *this*, etc as well as pronouns such as *they*, *his*, etc and make sure you know what they refer to. Look at extract **i**, line 2; *it* refers to CO_2, and in line 3, *They* refers to plants in the previous sentence. Look at extract **ii**; it is only clear that *ones* refers to *sources* when we look at the rest of the sentence and see that *oil sands* is an example of a source of fuel, not a fuel itself.

Understanding paraphrasing

Look at the way the extracts from the text below have been rewritten using different words (paraphrased). Is the meaning the same or different? If the meaning is different, change the paraphrase to make the meaning the same as the extract.

1	If governments adopt the right rules and incentives, by the middle of this century renewable sources will provide nearly 30 per cent of the world's energy.	*By implementing effective policies, governments can ensure that a third of energy production will come from alternative sources by 2050.*
2	Greater variety of fuel choices will be a boon for consumers. Different fuels will be stronger in different regions.	*The range of available fuels will expand, while their popularity will vary from country to country.*
3	Wind, solar and hydropower will account for 30 per cent of electricity generation by 2030, up from about 18 per cent today.	*By the third decade of the 21st century, sustainable energy sources will generate a third of our electricity, an increase of 12 per cent on current figures.*
4	Indeed, fossil fuels; coal, oil and natural gas, will continue to provide more than half the world's energy in 2050, building a long bridge to an era when alternatives can take over.	*As the process of converting to alternative energy sources will take a long time, non-renewable fuels will still account for over 50% of our global energy production in the middle of the 21st century.*

True, False or Not Given and Yes, No or Not Given

Do the following statements agree with the information given in Reading Passage 3? Write:

YES if the statement agrees with the information given
NO if the statement contradicts the information given
NOT GIVEN if there is no information about this

1 Renewable fuel sources will replace fossil fuels by the middle of the 21st century.
2 All hybrid cars will be able to recharge their batteries by connecting to the mains supply.
3 There will be at least twice as many cars on the roads by 2050.
4 Hydrogen is one of the lightest chemical elements.
5 Ethanol is produced in Brazil.
6 Nuclear power is a clean source of energy.

If your answer was *Yes* or *No*, underline the words in the passage which gave you the information.

Recognizing opinion

The reading passages in the IELTS exam often contain both fact and opinion.

1 Read statements **1–5** below. According to Reading Passage 3, which are facts and which are opinions? Write F for fact or O for opinion next to each statement.

1 In the future it will be possible to develop ecologically sustainable road transport. …………
2 Hybrid cars will account for 15 per cent of the new motor fleet in 2020. …………
3 Nearly half of Brazil's petrol is currently derived from sugar cane. …………
4 Governments will have to use financial methods to boost the production of alternative fuels. …………
5 Just 7 per cent of energy worldwide is generated from sustainable sources. …………

2 Match the items **1–4** below with the percentage contribution they are expected to make to fuel or energy production in the future.

1 fossil fuels
2 biofuels
3 electricity and petrol
4 renewable sources

A approximately 7 per cent
B more than 50 per cent
C maximum 15 per cent
D about 30 per cent
E maximum 10 per cent

3 In Reading Passage 3, the writer's main purpose is

1 to warn people of the dangers of fossil fuels.
2 to predict the future of energy and fuel sources.
3 to present different arguments on the subject of sustainable energy.
4 to describe the processes of generating low carbon fuels.

Skills practice

Now practise the skills you have learnt by answering the questions on Reading Passage 4.

Reading Passage 4

HOW TO FEED A HUNGRY WORLD

A Producing enough food for the world's population in 2050 will be easy. But doing it at an acceptable cost to the planet will depend on research into everything from high-tech seeds to low-tech farming practices.

B With the world's population expected to grow from 6.8 billion today to 9.1 billion by 2050, a certain Malthusian alarmism has set in: how will all these extra mouths be fed? The world's population more than doubled from 3 billion between 1961 and 2007, yet agricultural output kept pace – and current projections suggest it will continue to do so. Admittedly, climate change adds a large degree of uncertainty to projections of agricultural output, but that just underlines the importance of monitoring and research to refine those predictions. That aside, in the words of one official at the Food and Agriculture Organization (FAO) of the United Nations, the task of feeding the world's population in 2050 in itself seems 'easily possible'. Easy, that is, if the world brings into play swathes of extra land, spreads still more fertilizers and pesticides, and further depletes already scarce groundwater supplies. But clearing hundreds of millions of hectares of wildlands – most of the land that would be brought into use is in Latin America and Africa – while increasing today's brand of resource-intensive, environmentally destructive agriculture is a poor option. Therein lies the real challenge in the coming decades: how to expand agricultural output massively without increasing by much the amount of land used.

C What is needed is a second green revolution – an approach that Britain's Royal Society aptly describes as the 'sustainable intensification of global agriculture'. Such a revolution will require a wholesale realignment of priorities in agricultural research. There is an urgent need for fertilizers or other inputs – created, for example, through long neglected research on modifying roots – and for crops that are more resistant to drought, heat, submersion and pests. Equally crucial is lower tech research into basics such as crop rotation, mixed farming of animals and plants on smallholder farms, soil management and curbing waste. Between one-quarter and one-third of the food produced worldwide is lost or spoiled.

D Developing nations could score substantial gains in productivity by making better use of modern technologies and practices. But that requires money: the FAO estimates that to meet the 2050 challenge, investment throughout the agricultural chain in the developing world must double to US$83 billion a year. Most of that money needs to go towards improving agricultural infrastructure, from production to storage and processing. In Africa, the lack of roads also hampers agricultural productivity, making it expensive and difficult for farmers to get synthetic fertilizers. And research agendas need to be focused on the needs of the poorest and most resource-limited countries, where the majority of the world's population lives and where population growth over the next decades will be greatest. Above all, reinventing farming requires a multidisciplinary approach that involves not just biologists, agronomists and farmers, but also ecologists, policy-makers and social scientists.

E To their credit, the world's agricultural scientists are embracing such a broad view. In March, for example, they came together at the first Global Conference on Agricultural Research for Development in Montpellier, France, to begin working out how to realign research agendas to help meet the needs of farmers in poorer nations. But these plans will not bear fruit unless they get considerably more support from policy-makers and funders.

F The growth in public agricultural-research spending peaked in the 1970s and has been declining ever since. Today it is largely flat in rich nations and is actually decreasing in some countries in sub-Saharan Africa, where food needs are among the greatest. The big exceptions are China, where spending has grown exponentially over the past decade, and, to a lesser extent, India and Brazil. These three countries seem set to become the key suppliers of relevant science and technology to poorer countries. But rich countries have a responsibility too, and calls by scientists for large increases in public spending on agricultural research that is more directly relevant to the developing world are more than justified.

G The private sector also has an important part to play. In the past, agri-biotechnology companies have focused mostly on the lucrative agriculture markets in rich countries, where private-sector research accounts for more than half of all agricultural research. Recently, however, they have begun to engage in public-private partnerships to generate crops that meet the needs of poorer countries. This move mirrors the emergence more than a decade ago of public partnerships with drug companies to tackle a similar market failure: the development of drugs and vaccines for neglected diseases. As such, it is welcome, and should be greatly expanded.

Glossary

High-tech – using the most modern or advanced technology available

Robert Malthus (1776–1834) proposed the theory that the population is naturally controlled by cycles of disease and famine.

Alarmism – unnecessary worry or fear

Output – the amount of something that a person, organization, system, etc produces

Swathes – large areas of land

Realignment – reorganization of a system or institution

Drought – a long period of time when there is little or no rain and crops die

Smallholder – someone who owns a very small farm

Infrastructure – the set of systems within a place that affect how well it operates, for example the telephone and transport systems in a country

Exponentially – increasing or growing very fast

Agri-biotechnology – the science of genetically modifying plants to improve production

Lucrative – bringing a lot of money

Questions 1–4

Reading Passage 4 has seven paragraphs **A–G**. Which paragraphs include the following information? Write the appropriate letters.

1 The research on improving crop varieties and farming techniques. ....

2 Worldwide population data. ....

3 The involvement of the private sector in agricultural research. ....

4 Agricultural research investment patterns across the world. ....

Questions 5–8

Write **NO MORE THAN THREE WORDS AND/OR A NUMBER** for each answer.

5 What factor makes it more difficult to predict future agricultural production?

....

6 What proportion of food is wasted globally? ....

7 How much money does the developing world need for agriculture annually?

....

8 Which developing country has increased its spending on agricultural research the most? ....

Questions 9–12

Do the following statements agree with the information given in Reading Passage 4?
Write:

TRUE   if the statement is true according to the passage

FALSE   if the statement is false according to the passage

NOT GIVEN   if there is no information about this

9   Research into farming techniques is not as important as finding new crop varieties.
....

10 Improvements in farming methods depend on the collaboration of specialists from many different fields. ....

11 Future population growth will be higher in countries where there are fewest resources. ....

12 There is an urgent need for more qualified farmers in Africa.
....

Questions 13–18

Circle the correct letter, **A**, **B**, **C** or **D**.

13 Using more land for agriculture will ...
   A damage the environment.
   B spread disease.
   C be the best way to feed the growing population.
   D save water.

14 New crop varieties should ...
   A not increase food production.
   B be able to withstand extreme weather conditions.
   C use more fertilizers.
   D be rotated.

15 Improving rural transport in Africa will ...
   A improve storage facilities.
   B reduce productivity.
   C make it easier for farmers to use chemical fertilizers.
   D damage the infrastructure.

16 Three developing countries are investing in ...
   A further agricultural research.
   B new drugs.
   C poorer countries.
   D public spending.

17 The private sector has ...
   A already met the all food needs of poorer countries.
   B not yet formed partnerships with governments.
   C started to research into new crop technology for developing countries.
   D traditionally concentrated its research investment on products for poor countries.

18 The writer of the article thinks that ...
   A rich countries should provide poor countries with food.
   B agricultural research should focus on the needs of developing countries.
   C private companies should only fund research into profitable products.
   D modern technology is too complex to benefit developing countries.

Skills development

Summary completion

Read Passage 5 and complete the summary with words from the box. Note that there are more words than spaces, so you do not need to use them all.

majority	universities	employers	overseas	international	half	minority

Research into (1) .... study patterns has shown that, although UK (2) .... think highly of employees with overseas experience, a very small (3) .... of British students actually study abroad. (4) .... these students study at undergraduate level, while the other 50 per cent are on postgraduate programmes.

Glossary
Offset – to balance the effect of something

Reading Passage 5

GAIN OR DRAIN? HOW STUDY ABROAD AFFECTS OUR ECONOMY

A The number of British students enrolling at international universities is rising, but at what cost? Building broader networks and a greater diversity of experience enhances our position in the global economy, but it could also mean we're facing a 'brain drain' where our biggest and brightest talent floods out of the UK.

B 'A generation ago, going to university was seen as great preparation for life,' says Will Archer, CEO of the International Graduate Insight Group (i-graduate), an independent, global benchmarking and consultancy service. 'In today's and tomorrow's world, is limiting yourself to your national borders a preparation for living?'

C The British Council's position is clear: students should pack their bags and go. Simon Williams, the British Council's director of EU education programmes, says: 'We would encourage people to study abroad because we can see the great benefits, both on a personal and on a professional level.'

D Yet despite a number of British Council surveys showing that employers value international experience, students seem reluctant to leave. An estimated 33,000 UK citizens are currently undertaking higher education in other parts of the world, accounting for just 1.8 per cent of all UK students in higher education. These are divided equally between undergraduates and postgraduates, with roughly 0.9 per cent choosing to study abroad for some or all of their course at each level.

E Ronald Skeldon, a professorial fellow in the School of Global Studies at the University of Sussex, notes: 'It's difficult to assess the benefits of international study to us as a nation, because the numbers going are quite small, so the impact they might have on our economy or society would be very small.'

F Numbers of students coming in to the UK to study are high, however. Currently educating 370,000 international students, the UK comes second after the USA as a global study destination – although China, Denmark, Holland and Finland are fast encroaching on that territory. These are precious imports: a number of UK postgraduate science, technology and engineering courses could collapse without international students. In biotechnology, 93 per cent of students are international; in computer science it's 82 per cent; and in engineering subjects, nearly 90 per cent. 'We know that the UK is a net importer of foreign students,' says Williams. 'An interesting question would be: could any brain drain among UK postgraduates be offset – or maybe more than offset – by the 'brain gain' of postgraduates from other countries who come to study here and stay?'

G Outward mobility – the number of British students taking places at international universities – has become an area for research at the Higher Education Funding Council for England (HEFCE), the British Council, within universities, and for the Government. The Department for Business, Innovation and Skills, then under a different name, commissioned a study exploring the motivations and experiences of UK students studying abroad. The review involved 560 questionnaires completed by UK students living and studying in the USA, Ireland, Australia, France, Germany and the Czech Republic. The report suggests the notion of brain drain is ill-founded: 76 per cent of surveyed students planned to return.

H Fiona Smith, lecturer and researcher at the Centre for Applied Population Research at Dundee, worked on the report. 'About half of those we surveyed were engaged in postgraduate study, and half were in undergraduate study,' she explains. 'Interestingly, those with the highest qualifications were the most likely to intend to return to the UK, either after they completed their course, or after a short period of working abroad.' Smith adds that there was a distinction between those who were studying abroad in order to migrate – which happens a lot when it comes to studying in Australia – and those who wanted to access particular expertise to develop their career and their personal skills. 'Returning to the UK, for them, was part of that plan,' she says.

Guessing meaning from context

In the previous exercise we saw how a phrase from the text (*divided equally*) was replaced with a synonym (*half*) in the summary. When you come across a new word, you may find some clues to its meaning in the sentence(s) around it. Look at this sentence:

Building broader networks and a greater diversity of experience enhances our position in the global economy, but it could also mean we're facing a '**brain drain**' where our biggest and brightest **talent floods out of the UK.**

The two phrases *brain drain* and *talent floods out of the UK* together make it clear that the writer is describing **the flow of intelligence or skills away from Britain** and help you to guess the meaning of the phrase *brain drain*.

Remember
- Read all the notes or the whole summary first to check general understanding.
- Decide what kind of word or words you are looking for.
- Read the relevant section of the passage to find the words you need.
- Do not use your own words.

1 Look at Reading Passage 5 again and find words which mean the same as definitions **1–6** below.

1 improves
2 urge
3 effect
4 expanding into
5 final, after making all deductions
6 away from the centre/base

2 Underline the other words in the text which helped you guess correctly.

Note completion

Notes often list key points about the passage or part of a passage.

Complete the notes below. Choose **ONE OR TWO WORDS** from Reading Passage 5 paragraph H for each answer.

Remember
- Find the section of the passage that the notes refer to (normally in the same order as the questions) and find words or phrases which have the same meaning as the sentence you have to complete. Looking for synonyms may help.
- If you have to complete the notes from words in a box, check that the word forms are grammatically possible.
- If you have to complete the notes by choosing words from the passage yourself, make sure you use the right number of words and that your answer is logical and grammatically correct.

According to Fiona Smith, the students who had the (1) .... were the most interested in returning to the UK.

Some students were studying in Australia because they wanted to (2) ...., but others were more interested in acquiring specific (3) ....

Understanding paraphrasing and sentence completion

1 Look back at paragraphs **A–E** of Reading Passage 5 and find phrases or sentences with the same meaning as **1–5** below.

1 interacting with a wider range of social groups
2 staying in your own country
3 take the opportunity to travel
4 studying at university
5 to calculate the advantages of overseas education

2 Look at paragraphs **E–H** and choose **ONE** phrase from **A–F** below to complete sentences **1–3**.

1 In the survey of UK students studying overseas, the students with the best grades ...
2 Many science and engineering programmes at UK universities ...
3 The number of UK students studying abroad ...

List of phrases

A were planning to migrate.	**D** is statistically insignificant.
B were expecting to return to the UK.	**E** are expanding into Europe.
C rely on international enrolments for their survival.	**F** will increase in the future.

3 Complete the sentences below with words from Reading Passage 5, paragraphs **A–D**. Write **NO MORE THAN THREE WORDS OR A NUMBER** for each answer.

1 There is a rising trend for UK students to continue their education

....

2 It is important for students to expand their experience beyond their

....

3 The advantages of an international education can be appreciated on an individual and ....

4 The majority of UK students are .... in spite of the employment advantages they could gain from studying abroad.

Skills practice

Now practise the skills you have learnt by answering the questions on Reading Passage 6.

Reading Passage 6

GENETIC INEQUALITY: HUMAN GENETIC ENGINEERING

As genetics allows us to turn the tide on human disease, it's also granting the power to engineer desirable traits into humans. What limits should we put on this technology?

A Genes influence health and disease, as well as human traits and behavior. Researchers are just beginning to use genetic technology to unravel the genomic contributions to these different phenotypes, and as they do so, they are also discovering a variety of other potential applications for this technology. For instance, ongoing advances make it increasingly likely that scientists will someday be able to genetically engineer humans to possess certain desired traits. Of course, the possibility of human genetic engineering raises numerous ethical and legal questions. Although such questions rarely have clear and definite answers, the expertise and research of bioethicists, sociologists, anthropologists, and other social scientists can inform us about how different individuals, cultures, and religions view the ethical boundaries for the uses of genomics. Moreover, such insights can assist in the development of guidelines and policies.

B Over the years, the desire for better sports performance has driven many trainers and athletes to abuse scientific research in an attempt to gain an unfair advantage over their competitors. Historically, such efforts have involved the use of performance-enhancing drugs that were originally meant to treat people with disease. This practice is called doping, and it frequently involved such substances as erythropoietin, steroids, and growth hormones (Filipp, 2007). To control this drive for an unfair competitive edge, in 1999, the International Olympic® Committee created the World Anti-Doping Agency (WADA), which prohibits the use of performance-enhancing drugs by athletes. WADA also conducts various testing programs in an attempt to catch those athletes who violate the anti-doping rules.

C Today, WADA has a new hurdle to overcome – that of gene doping. This practice is defined as the nontherapeutic use of cells, genes, or genetic elements to enhance athletic performance. Gene doping takes advantage of cutting-edge research in gene therapy that involves the transfer of genetic material to human cells to treat or prevent disease (Well, 2008). Because gene doping increases the amount of proteins and hormones that cells normally make, testing for genetic performance enhancers will be very difficult, and a new race is on to develop ways to detect this form of doping (Baoutina et al., 2008).

D Genetic testing also harbors the potential for yet another scientific strategy to be applied in the area of eugenics, or the social philosophy of promoting the improvement of inherited human traits through intervention. In the past, eugenics was used to justify practices including involuntary sterilization and euthanasia. Today, many people fear that preimplantation genetic diagnosis may be perfected and could technically be applied to select specific nondisease traits (rather than eliminate severe disease, as it is currently used) in implanted embryos, thus amounting to a form of eugenics. In the media, this possibility has been sensationalized and is referred to as 'designer babies', an expression that has been included in the Oxford English Dictionary. Although possible, this genetic technology has not yet been implemented; but it continues to bring up many heated ethical issues.

Glossary
Genetic – related to genes, the cells of living organisms
Traits – particular qualities in someone's character
Phenotypes – the qualities of a living thing that result from how its genes and the environment affect each other
Genomics – the study of genetic and environmental factors in disease
Steroids – a chemical that is produced in the body or made as a drug
Nontherapeutic – not helping to treat or cure illness
Eugenics – the idea that society can be improved by only allowing people to produce healthy and intelligent children
Euthanasia – the practice of ending someone's life without causing pain
Preimplantation – before a human embryo is placed in the uterus

Questions 1–4

Complete the summary below with words from the box. You do not need to use all the words.

| political | genetics | performance | engineering | ethical | characteristics |
| anthropology | personality |

Advances in the study of (1) .... have made it probable that, in the future, not only will it be possible to scientifically manipulate physical (2) .... before birth but also certain aspects of human (3) .... The (4) .... aspects of this potential are highly controversial.

Questions 5–8

Complete the summary below. Choose **ONE** word from paragraph **B** of Reading Passage 6 for each answer.

Some genetically based (5) ...., intended for medical purposes, can be used to improve (6) .... performance. (7) .... gives athletes an unfair advantage and is not allowed by the International Olympic® Committee. The (8) .... are enforced through a series of drug-testing systems.

Questions 9–12

Choose one phrase from **A–G** below to complete sentences **9–12**.

9 Eugenics is the belief ...

10 Currently, embryos can be analysed genetically ...

11 In the future, embryos could be scientifically manipulated to produce ...

12 There is widespread debate about the ethics of modifying genes ...

List of phrases
A for commercial profit.
B to produce particular human traits.
C to diagnose behavioural problems.
D to detect serious diseases.
E that it is unethical to modify human genes.
F specific physical or behavioural characteristics.
G that the human race can be improved through genetic modification.

Questions 13–16

Complete each of the statements below with words from Reading Passage 6. Write **NO MORE THAN THREE WORDS** for each answer.

13 .... is a scientific method of analysing the effect of genes on human characteristics.

14 Multidisciplinary research into genomics can contribute to the planning of
....

15 Athletes are forbidden to use .... drugs when they compete in the Olympic® Games.

16 Gene therapy involves transferring .... from one person to another for medical purposes.

How much do you know about the IELTS Academic Writing module?
Do the quiz below to find out.

Quiz

1 How long (minutes) is the Writing module?
   A 90   **B** 60   **C** 50

2 Complete the table.

	How long should you spend on this task?	Minimum number of words
Task 1		
Task 2		

3 In Task 1 what do you have to do?
   A present your opinions
   B describe visual data
   C write a story

4 In Task 2 what do you have to do?
   A present and justify your opinions
   B describe a historical event
   C compare and contrast photographs

Writing Task 1

In Task 1 you will be asked to describe visual data, for example a chart, graph or table in at least 150 words.

Skills development
Understanding data

1 In figures **1–4** identify:

   1 a line graph
   2 a bar chart
   3 a table
   4 a pie chart

2 In labels **A–F** identify:

   1 a vertical axis
   2 a horizontal axis
   3 a column
   4 a row
   5 a segment showing just over a tenth
   6 a segment showing just under a tenth

Figure 1

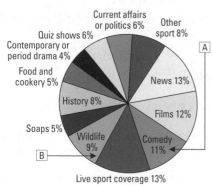

Selected types of television programmes viewed by men: 2007/08

Figure 2

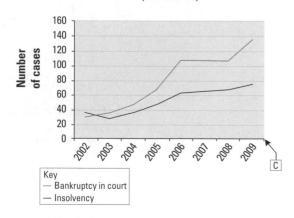

Debt in England and Wales (thousands)

Key
— Bankruptcy in court
— Insolvency

Figure 3

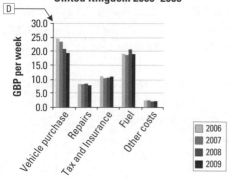

Household expenditure on motoring in real terms United Kingdom 2006–2009

2006
2007
2008
2009

Figure 4

Population age structure
United Kingdom percentages

	1971	1991	2001	2008	2031
85 and over	1	2	2	2	4
65 to 84	12	14	14	14	18
16 to 64	61	64	64	65	60
Under 16	25	20	20	19	18

3 Which figure **1–4** tells you about:

   1 the percentage of the population by age?
   2 the trend of debt in two parts of the UK?
   3 how much people spend on owning and running a car?
   4 how many people watch the news?

4 Look at figures **1–4** again and find the answers to these questions.

Figure 1	1	What type of television programme was least popular in 2007/08?
	2	Which programmes were most popular in 2007/08?
Figure 2	1	How many people were declared bankrupt in 2002?
	2	In what year did insolvency decrease?
Figure 3	1	What was the most expensive motoring item in 2006?
	2	In what year was fuel the most expensive item?
Figure 4	1	What does the first column of statistics refer to?
	2	What does the row at the bottom refer to?

Language focus: Expressing figures and quantities

1 Now complete these sentences. Refer to figures **1–4**.

   1 In 2007–08, over .... of programmes viewed by men were news, films, comedy and sport, in comparison with cookery and soaps which accounted for only ....
   2 Bankruptcy in court increased from about 28,000 cases in .... to approximately 134,000 cases in ....
   3 The cost of buying a car fell from 23 GBP per week in .... to 19.5 GBP in ....
   4 In 1971 .... of the population in the UK was under 16, whereas by .... it had fallen to 19 per cent.

2 Complete the sentences below with a phrase from the box. Refer to figures **1–4**.

much more	exactly the same	more than trebled	very little	half as many
	a quarter	twice as many	slightly more	

   1 Viewing figures for current affairs programmes and quiz shows were .... in 2007 and 2008.
   2 Men viewed .... history programmes as contemporary drama.
   3 From 2002 to 2009, bankruptcies rose .... than insolvencies.
   4 In 2009, bankruptcies .... those in 2002.
   5 In 2008, fuel was .... expensive than in other years.
   6 Tax and insurance costs changed .... between 2006 and 2008.
   7 In 1971, the number of people aged 85 and over was .... of the number predicted for 2031.
   8 In 1971, there were less than .... people aged 65–84 as people under 16.

The opening statement

Here is a sample outline of a Task 1 answer:

- opening statement
- general information and most significant trends
- more specific information and evidence of significant trends
- concluding overview, summarizing the key information (for a higher score)

1 Look at the bar chart. Which of the sentences **A–D** below is the most appropriate opening statement? Why?

Figure 5

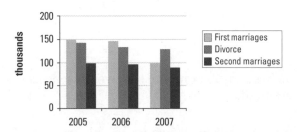

Marriages and Divorces in the United Kingdom

A This bar chart shows the number of marriages and divorces in the UK.
B This bar chart proves that weddings are not as popular as they used to be and people often get married when they are older.
C This chart shows falling trends in the number of first marriages, divorces and remarriages in the UK in the period 2005–2007.
D The chart clearly illustrates that the number of first marriages has risen and the number of divorces is at a similar level.

2 Sometimes Task 1 requires you to write a report about two diagrams. In this case you need to write an opening statement which comments on both sets of data.

   1 Which of the statements below is most appropriate for the bar chart?

Figure 6

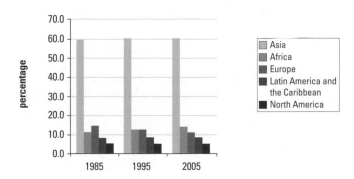

Selected regions and share of world population

A The percentage share of the world population rose in the developing regions between 1985 and 2005 in contrast with Europe and North America, where it decreased slightly.
B The percentage share of the world population in Europe was the same as Africa's in 1995.

2 Which of the statements below is most appropriate for the line graph?
  A While China's share of the world population declined between the 20th and 21st centuries, India's share increased.
  B Between 1985 and 2005, India's percentage share of the population rose, in contrast with that of China and the European Union, which both decreased.

Figure 7

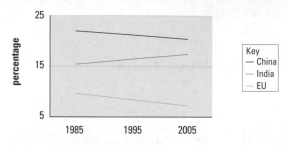

Selected countries' and regions' share of world population

3 Now find the best way to combine the two sentences you chose in exercise 2 in an opening statement.

Language focus: Describing change over a period of time

The main aim of Writing Task 1 is to describe information shown in diagrams.

1 Look at the diagrams below. Match the phrases to the appropriate diagram.

increased sharply   fluctuated   fell gradually   remained stable

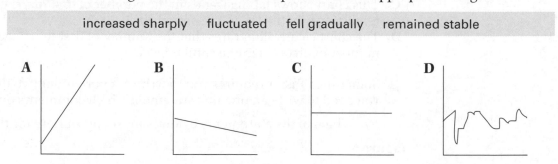

2 Look at the phrases below. Match them to the phrases in exercise 1. Not all of the phrases will match.

Example: *increased sharply* – rose dramatically

reached a peak   rose dramatically   decreased steadily   varied   stayed the same
increased gradually   fell slightly

3 Read the paragraph below which describes the bar chart. <u>Underline</u> the verbs and say why each tense is used.

The bar chart shows that between 1985 and 2005 the percentage share of the world population rose in developing regions such as Africa and Asia, while it decreased in regions such as Europe and North America. Asia's proportion of the population remained the highest throughout the two decades, at approximately 60 per cent.

Figure 8

Selected regions and share of world population

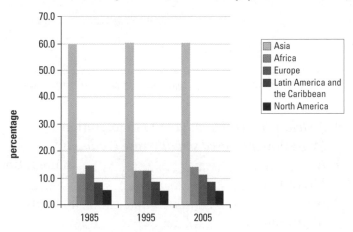

4 Choose the best alternative from the words in *italics*.

In Latin America there was a (1) *same/similar* trend where the percentage (2) *remained relatively stable/stayed exactly the same* at around 8 per cent while the North American percentage share remained the (3) *lowest/little* over the period at approximately 5 per cent. After Asia, Europe and Africa had the (4) *second highest/ next proportion* of the population. While Europe's share of the population fell (5) *sharply/gradually* over the 20 years, Africa's share (6) *rose dramatically/ increased slightly* from 11 per cent to 14 per cent and in 2005 it overtook Europe to take second place to Asia.

5 Read the text and complete the gaps with an appropriate word or phrase from the box.

> rose progressively   decreasing steadily   consistently   highest   just under
> downward trend

> The line graph shows the percentage share of the population in three regions; China, India and Europe, between 1985 and 2005. In 1985, China's share of the world population was the (1) .... at 22 per cent, India followed with 16 per cent and Europe with (2) .... 10 per cent. Over the twenty years, although China's share was (3) .... the highest, there was a (4) ...., with the proportion falling to 20 per cent in 2005. Europe showed a similar pattern with its share (5) .... to approximately 7 per cent in the same year. In contrast, India's share (6) .... to nearly 18 per cent in 2005, bringing its population share very close to that of China.

6 Look at the line graph below and complete the gaps using an appropriate phrase to describe the changes shown.

Figure 9

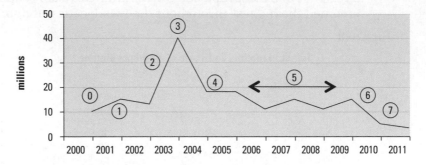

Migration trends 2000 to 2011

0 A *steady increase/gradual rise* in migration
Migration *increased steadily/rose gradually.*

1 A.................................... .... in migration.
Migration ....

2 A.................................... .... in migration.
Migration ....

3 Migration .... in 2003.

4 Migration ....

5 Migration ....

6 A.................................... .... in migration.
Migration ....

7 A.................................... .... in migration.
Migration ....

Skills practice

Now practise the skills you have learnt by studying the diagram and writing four sentences to describe the information shown.

Figure 10

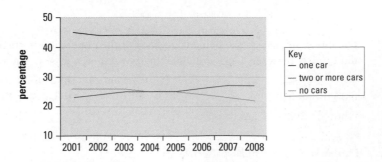

Households with regular use of a car in Great Britain

Study Skills: Writing

Skills development

Selecting and grouping key information

1 Study the bar charts. Then read the six statements **A–F** below. Choose the three statements that best represent the most important information from the charts.

Top ten active sports: by sex 2007/08

Figure 11

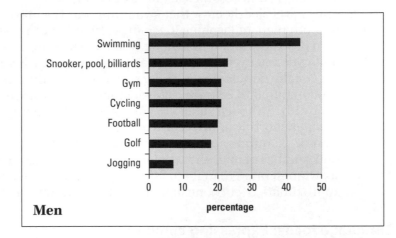

Men

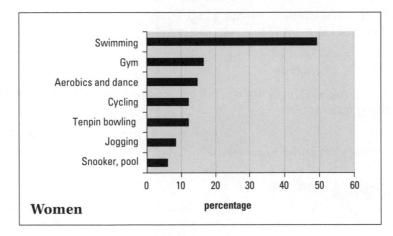

Women

A Swimming is the most popular sport for men and women.
B The same number of men (21 per cent) said they liked going to the gym and cycling.
C Snooker is the least popular sport for women.
D Cycling is as popular as tenpin bowling for women.
E Jogging is the least popular sport for men.
F Aerobics and dance are the third most popular sports for women.

2 Look at the bar charts above again. Read the six statements **A–F** below and choose the three that best show how to group key information from both charts.

A Both men and women swim.
B Swimming and gym are very popular sports for men and women.
C 22 per cent of women and 21 per cent of men interviewed go to the gym.
D Snooker is the second most popular sport for men, but the least popular for women.
E Swimming is more popular with women than men, whereas the opposite is true of cycling.
F Golf is popular with men, whereas tenpin bowling is popular with women.

3 Now read parts of three sample answers for the bar charts in exercise 1. Which do you think is the best answer and why?

A Swimming is the most popular sport for men (44) and women (49). Pool and billiards are the second most popular sports for men (23) but very few women are interested in them (7). Gym is the third most popular sport for men (21) and the second most popular for women (17). Jogging is the least popular sport for men (7) and second least for women (8).

B The charts clearly show that swimming was the most popular sporting activity for both men and women (over 40 per cent in both cases), whereas very few men or women enjoyed jogging (7 and 8 per cent respectively). It is also evident that gym and cycling are popular with both sexes. For men cycling and gym are equally popular (with 21 per cent) and slightly more popular than football (21 compared to 20), while considerably more women use the gym than cycle (17 to 13). Although snooker is men's second favourite sport, it was the least popular sporting activity for women.

C First of all, number of men play snooker are 3 times more than women. And number of men and woman like to swimming are similar, just around six woman more than men. Secondly, number of men like to cycling are approximate twenty one men more than woman which is just 12.

Language focus: Expressing comparison and contrast

Remember
Include a range of different expressions to compare or contrast data in your answer.

Find seven examples of language from the best sample answer which compares or contrasts the data shown in the charts.

Skills practice

Now practise the skills you have learnt by looking at the chart below and answering the questions.

Figure 12

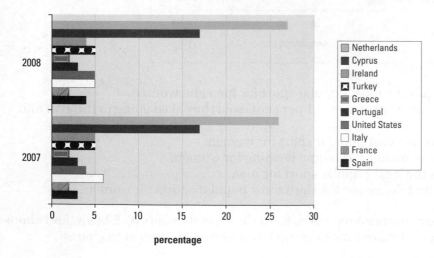

UK residents' holiday visits abroad: by destination

percentage

Legend: Netherlands, Cyprus, Ireland, Turkey, Greece, Portugal, United States, Italy, France, Spain

1 Look at the chart showing statistics for **UK** passengers travelling to other countries and answer the questions below.

  1 What does this bar chart show?
  2 What does the vertical axis represent?
  3 What does the horizontal axis represent?
  4 What do each of the shaded columns represent?
  5 What are the most significant features in this diagram?

2 Read the sample answer below. Underline the key information and circle connecting words.

  What can you say about:
  • the length?
  • the style?

From the bar charts it's easy to see most of the UK residents go on international holidays to netherlands in 2007 and 2008. Ten country had been researched and we can see that cyprus is in second place both years.

turkey and ireland is equal popular in 2007, but Ireland visitors were not so many in 2008 and 2007. However the same number of tourist visit Turkey in this years. In 2007 Italy was the third more popular destination with 6 per cent, but is decreased to 5 per cent in 2008, the same as United states. Tourist to France is the same in 2007 and 2008.

The data also shows that tourism to Netherlands is 3 or 4 times higher than others countries both in 2007 and 2008. In the two years, it has been increased slight.

3 Check and correct the grammar, vocabulary and spelling.

Skills development

Describing a process

Read the statements below. They describe the different stages in the enrolment procedure for a person who wants to do an English course at a language school or college.

- ☐ The student pays the fees for the course.
- ☐ The student's details are put on the computer.
- ☐ The student goes to the institution and completes a placement test.
- ☐ The student has now enrolled and is given a student card.
- ☐ The student is placed in a class at the appropriate level.
- ☐ The student contacts the institution about the English course.
- ☐ The student is interviewed by an experienced teacher.
- ☐ The necessary forms are completed.

1 Which are the first and final stages of this process?

2 Number the sentences in a logical order.

3 <u>Underline</u> the verbs in each sentence. Are they active or passive? Which tenses are used?

4 Choose the best introduction for this enrolment procedure from **A–C**.

   A The procedure for this activity is as follows:
   B The procedure for improving your English at a language school or college is as follows:
   C The procedure for enrolling for an English course at a language school or college is as follows:

5 Choose an appropriate linking word and verb to complete each part of this description of an everyday activity.

after a few minutes	then	after that	finally	next	~~first of all~~

add	pour	drink	~~boil~~	put	take out

0 *first of all boil* .... the water.
1 .... a teabag into a cup.
2 .... the boiling water into the cup.
3 .... the teabag.
4 .... some milk and sugar and stir.
5 .... the tea.

6 Now add appropriate sequencing words to the sentences about enrolling on an English course to give the passage more cohesion, e.g. ***first of all***, ***then***, ***finally***, etc.

Skills practice

Now practise the skills you have learnt by looking at the diagram below about how waste paper is recycled to make better quality paper.

1 Complete the diagram by matching each of the phrases below to a particular stage in the process.
   a Package product and send to customer
   b Pass through heavy roller to squeeze out water
   c Press and flatten into thin strips
   d Cut into sheets
   e Sort into categories (e.g. newspapers, copy paper, magazines)

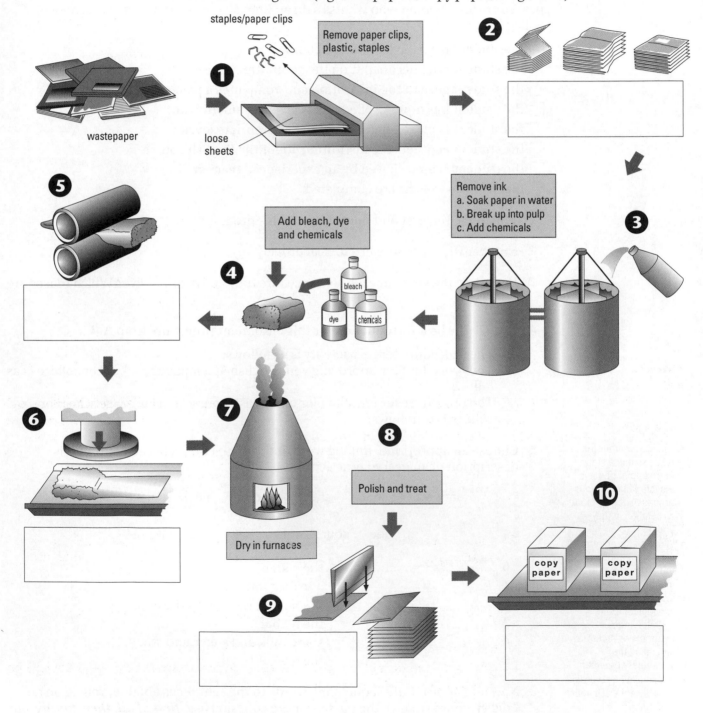

2 Now write a description of the process. Use an appropriate tense, use the passive form where necessary, and add appropriate linking words.

Skills development

Understanding the instructions and the question

IELTS Writing Task 2 questions usually include the following statements:

- You should spend about 40 minutes on this task.
- Present a written argument or case to an educated reader with no specialist knowledge of the following topic.
- Use your own ideas, knowledge and experience and support your arguments with examples and relevant evidence.

1 Decide if these statements are True or False.

    A You must spend exactly 40 minutes on this task.
    B To write about the topics, you need general rather than specialist knowledge.
    C You don't need to include your opinions.
    D You should present a clear argument giving examples and reasons.
    E Your writing should be in an informal, personal style.

Writing Task 2 questions usually include at least one of the following questions:

1 To what extent do you agree or disagree with this statement?
2 Do you agree?
3 What can be done about (a problem)?
4 Give reasons for your answer and include any relevant examples from your knowledge or experience.
5 Discuss both points of view and give your opinion.

2 Match each of the questions above to these instructions.

    A Explain why you hold a specific view
    B Present both sides of the argument
    C Give your personal views
    D Give your opinion and show that you understand other points of view
    E Suggest a solution to a problem

Understanding the topic and the task

Remember

- Make sure you understand what the topic or subject of the question is. Underline key words if necessary.
- Read the question carefully to identify exactly what you need to do.
- Focus on the question itself, not on what you want to write about.

Answer these questions.

Settling into a new culture can be extremely difficult. Although some 'culture shock' is inevitable, there are a number of ways to make living overseas much easier. What can be done to reduce culture shock?

1 What is the main topic?
    A Visiting foreign countries and new cultures.
    B The difficulties of studying overseas.
    C Adapting to life in a new country.

2 What is the task?
    A Suggest ways to reduce the effects of 'culture shock'.
    B Write about the advantages of living overseas.
    C Give reasons why living in the UK is more difficult than living in other countries.

Skills practice

Now practise the skills you have learnt by analysing the following essay titles.

1 Identify the topics and tasks for these questions.

    1 *One of the most serious problems that cities now face is crime. What can be done to prevent the spread of urban crime?*

    Main topic:

    Task:

2 *The effects of increased global tourism are more likely to be harmful than beneficial. Discuss both points of view and give your opinion.*

Main topic:

Task:

3 *Using animals to test the safety of cosmetics or drugs used for medical reasons is never acceptable. To what extent do you agree with this statement?*

Main topic:

Task:

In the IELTS Writing Task 2, candidates will be assessed on their ability to:

i present the solution to a problem
ii present and justify an opinion or evaluate and challenge ideas
iii compare and contrast evidence and opinions

2 Find the verbs in statements i–iii above that mean:
- to consider how things are different and how they are similar
- to show a good reason for something
- to compare two things to show how they are different
- to question whether something is true or accurate

3 Now match statements i–iii to questions **1–3** on pages 47–48.

Brainstorming and planning

Remember
- You must write at least the number of words specified or you will lose marks.
- You will not have time to count words in the exam, so count words when you are practising so you know roughly how much to write.

1 Look at the question about settling into a new culture. Then decide where to put the items in the table. The first one has been done for you as an example.

Settling into a new culture can be extremely difficult. Although some 'culture shock' is inevitable, there are a number of ways to make living overseas much easier. What can be done to reduce culture shock?

> keep in contact with friends/family   people   ~~language~~   culture and lifestyle
> accommodation   find out about the place before you go
> try and meet/speak to local people   food and drink   religion
> join a club or society   sample local food   observe/respect local customs
> miss friends/family   ~~learn the language~~

Problems of living overseas	Ways to make living overseas easier
language	learn the language

2 Can you add one more point to each column in the table?

Remember
- It is important to generate ideas as quickly as possible.
- Use mindmaps and lists to organize information quickly.

Another way of organizing your ideas is through a mindmap. For example:

3 Now decide which you think are the three greatest difficulties when settling into a new culture.

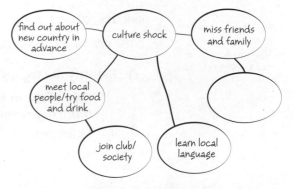

4 Look at the three diagrams below. Which is the most appropriate length for each section of a Task 2 answer?

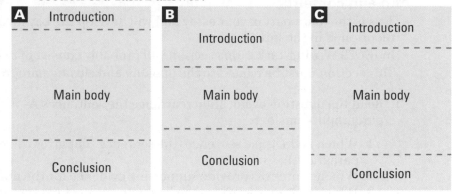

5 Which would be the best overall structure for this question?

Settling into a new culture can be extremely difficult. Although some 'culture shock' is inevitable, there are a number of ways to make living overseas much easier. What can be done to reduce culture shock?

A
Para. 1 – Intro: main difficulties of living overseas
Para. 2 – Examples of inevitable culture shock
Para. 3 – Suggestions on how to reduce culture shock
Para. 4 – Summary/conclusion of points above

B
Para. 1 – Intro: living and working overseas
Para. 2 – Examples of positive points of living overseas
Para. 3 – Examples of negative points of living overseas
Para. 4 – Summary of your opinion

C
Para. 1 – Intro: why you enjoy living overseas
Para. 2 – Reasons why people live overseas
Para. 3 – Suggestions on best places to live and study overseas

THE INTRODUCTION

Aim and contents

- A good introduction includes a general statement about the topic and says what the purpose of the essay is.
- It may also include the initial views of the writer on this subject – views that will be developed later.
- An introduction must be clear and relevant.

Which of the introductions below is most appropriate for this question. Why?

Settling into a new culture can be extremely difficult. Although some 'culture shock' is inevitable, there are a number of ways to make living overseas much easier. What can be done to reduce culture shock?

1 *Settling into a new culture can be very difficult. Although some 'culture shock' is inevitable, there are many ways to make living abroad easier.*

2 *I really enjoy living abroad but sometimes it is very hard and I miss my friends and family. I have been living in the UK for two years now and the best thing about it is learning English. However, the weather is awful and I really hate the food!*

3 *People move overseas to live, study or work for many different reasons. Although this can be a very positive experience there will often be difficulties to overcome. These problems might include getting used to living in a different culture, not knowing the language or simply missing friends and family.*

Aim and contents

- This is the main part of your essay and will develop the key ideas and topic mentioned in the introduction.
- In IELTS Writing Task 2, this section will probably consist of two or three paragraphs.
- This section must be related to the opening and closing paragraphs.

1 Read the question again. Then rearrange the sentences **A–F** below to make a clear paragraph. Consider:

    1 Which is the topic sentence (the sentence that gives the main idea of this paragraph)?
    2 Which sentences provide supporting evidence for the main idea?
    3 Which sentence provides the link with the next paragraph?

Settling into a new culture can be extremely difficult. Although some 'culture shock' is inevitable, there are a number of ways to make living overseas much easier. What can be done to reduce culture shock?

    A Not being able to speak the language very well can make life even more difficult.
    B However, there are a number of ways to reduce the difficulties.
    C Adjusting to a new culture can often take weeks or months.
    D In addition, other problems may arise from different lifestyles, types of food or accommodation.
    E During this period it is not uncommon for people to feel very homesick and really miss their friends and family.
    F There is no doubt that living overseas can be very difficult at times.

2 Now write the first paragraph of the main body of your answer using sentences **A–F** above.

3 Put the linking words in the box in the appropriate place in the table. Then add one more word for each column.

> ~~in addition~~   because   secondly   therefore   finally   besides   ~~however~~
> despite this   so   although   ~~firstly~~   moreover   ~~as a result~~

Sequencers	Reason or result	Contrast	Extra information
firstly	as a result	however	in addition

4 Choose an appropriate linking word from the box to complete the paragraph.

(1).., it is a good idea to find as much information as possible before you move to another country by reading books or searching the internet. (2)..., speak to other people who have lived abroad and discuss their experiences. (3)..., it is important to learn the language and (4)... taking lessons is advisable. When you are living in a new country, if possible, try and make friends with local people (5)... you do not become lonely or isolated. (6)..., it is useful to keep in contact with people from your own country too. (7)...aim to be open-minded about the whole experience.

5 What are the four suggestions given in this paragraph about how to reduce 'culture shock'?

Remember
Use linking words to give your writing cohesion.

6 Improve the information by using an appropriate linking word. The first one has been done for you as an example.

0 The city centre flat was very expensive. A lot of traffic noise could be heard. (*Extra information*)

The city centre flat was very expensive. In addition/Moreover, a lot of traffic noise could be heard.

1 Many women have successful careers nowadays. Compared to men, not many women have senior positions. (*Contrast*)

2 In England I live with a host family. My spoken English has improved rapidly. (*Result*)

3 Many students go overseas to study. They believe the quality of education is higher. (*Reason*)

CONCLUSION

Aim and contents

The concluding paragraph sums up the key points covered in the essay.

1 Read the question again and choose the best conclusion for it from **A–C** below. Give your reasons.

Settling into a new culture can be extremely difficult. Although some 'culture shock' is inevitable, there are a number of ways to make living overseas much easier. What can be done to reduce culture shock?

A *Last but not least, living abroad is very difficult.*

B *Although living abroad results in inevitable problems, it is clear that a number of strategies could be useful in preventing many of these difficulties. If this advice is taken, the experience is likely to be far more positive.*

C *To sum up, here's my advice to you. Try and learn a language, speak to local people and follow local habits and traditions. I'm sure if you do this you'll be fine and everything will be great. That's all.*

Remember
• The conclusion must refer back to the points made in the essay. Don't include new information.
• The conclusion can sum up your views but should be written in an impersonal, academic style.

2 Use the words below to write a different conclusion for this question.

In/conclusion/settling/new/country/cause/problems
Some/difficulties/cannot/avoided/example ...
However/there/solutions/such as ...
Living/abroad/often/positive/experience/enjoy/possible

....
....
....
....

Skills practice

1   Go back to the answer to Question 1 on page 47 to check what the topic and the task were for this question:

   One of the most serious problems that cities now face is crime. What can be done to prevent the spread of urban crime?

   Topic:

   Task:

2   Brainstorm ideas for the question above. Use the table to make notes.

Other problems in cities	Crimes	Ways to prevent/reduce
congestion	*murder*	*more police*

3   Suggest an outline for the question.

   Paragraph 1 ....
   Paragraph 2 ....
   Paragraph 3 ....
   Paragraph 4 ....
   Paragraph 5 ....

4   Choose the best topic sentence A, B or C for the introduction below.

   A *Crime is a really big problem in all cities.*
   B *There is no doubt that numerous problems exist in most modern cities.*
   C *Nowadays crime is more important than any other city problem.*

   Although traffic congestion, pollution and overcrowding often occur, many people believe that crime is the most serious problem in urban areas. Indeed, television and newspaper reports often tell us that crime continues to rise. However, it is possible to tackle this serious issue in a number of ways.

5   In the first paragraph of the main body, you could say that your first solution to reduce crime would be to increase the number of police. Write a suitable topic sentence below.

   ....

   If more police were on the streets, whether on foot or in patrol cars, criminals would be less likely to commit crimes and people would feel much safer. Having more police visible at night would be particularly beneficial.

6 In the next paragraph, the topic sentence is given. Write two or three supporting sentences.

A second possibility would be to make laws stricter and punishments more severe.

....

....

....

....

....

7 In the next paragraph, number the sentences in the correct order.

☐ *This would reduce burglary and theft.*

☐ *Thirdly, methods to increase security might deter potential criminals.*

☐ *In terms of personal safety, rape alarms or even small weapons could prevent some attacks on people.*

☐ *For example, more effective alarms in houses and cars.*

☐ *In addition, more information about home security would also be useful.*

8 Choose an appropriate word or phrase from the box to complete the gaps in the final paragraph.

increased do however would are ways reduced although
in addition methods

In conclusion, (1) .... crime is a major problem in most cities in the world, the situation can be addressed by adopting the (2) .... mentioned above. In this way, the negative effects could be (3) .... and people living in cities (4) .... feel much safer.

Now check the model answer on page 82.

Further practice

You should spend about 40 minutes on this task.

Present a written argument or case to an educated reader with no specialist knowledge of the following topic:

Using animals to test the safety of cosmetics or drugs used for medical reasons is never acceptable. To what extent do you agree with this statement?

You should write at least 250 words.

Use your own ideas, knowledge and experience and support your arguments with examples and with relevant evidence.

Study Skills: Speaking

How much do you know about the IELTS Speaking module?

Do the quiz below to find out.

1 How long is the Speaking module?
   A 15–20 minutes
   B 11–14 minutes
   C 40–45 minutes

2 There are three main parts of the Speaking module. Are these statements about the three parts true or false?

Part 1

1 This part lasts between four and five minutes.
2 The candidate is asked to describe a picture.
3 The candidate answers general questions about themselves, their families, their jobs and other familiar topics.

Part 2

4 The candidate is given a minute to prepare to talk about a topic.
5 The candidate is asked to talk about a topic for ten minutes.
6 The candidate must choose what topic they wish to discuss.

Part 3

7 This part lasts between four and five minutes.
8 This part is a discussion between the candidate and examiner on a topic related to Part 2.
9 This is the easiest part of the module.

Part 1

Talking about familiar topics

In Part 1 of the Speaking module, you have to answer questions about familiar topics. You can't know exactly what you will be asked, but you can prepare.

Look at the topics below. Write questions that the examiner might ask you about them. Then look at the suggestions on page 82.

- Your studies
- Your previous work experience, your current job or your future career plans
- Your family/home life
- Your country
- Your hobbies and interests

Giving a good answer

1 Read some possible questions and answers for Part 1. Tick the answers that you think are good.

A **Examiner:** Who was your favourite teacher at school? Why did you like their lessons?
Candidate: Mr Wallis. Because they were easy.

B **Examiner:** How long have you been studying English?
Candidate: I am very interested in English because it is a world language and I hope it will help me to do well in my career.

C **Examiner:** What do you do?
Candidate: Well, at the moment I'm studying full time, but back in my country I'm a doctor and I hope to be able to find work here as a doctor too.

D **Examiner:** What are the best things about your job?
Candidate: Oh, definitely the people. I love meeting people from all over the world.

E **Examiner:** Do you live with your family?
Candidate: No.

F **Examiner:** How long have you been in the UK?
Candidate: I will stay three years.

G **Examiner:** Tell me about where you are living at the moment.
Candidate: It is a, er, er, what is the word, er, er, maisonette!

H **Examiner:** Do you enjoy travelling?
Candidate: Yes, I'm really interested in seeing the world. While I've been living in Britain I've also taken the opportunity to go to Europe and see France and Spain. I found the people in Spain really friendly.

2 How can you improve the other answers?

3 Now record yourself answering the same questions. Listen to the recording and evaluate your performance.

Remember

- Including short phrases about time or possibility in your answers can make them sound more fluent. e.g. *at the moment, recently, probably, definitely …*
- Other conversational expressions like *well, let me see, actually …* also make your speech sound more natural.

Useful language

At the moment I'm living/studying/working …
Before that I lived in …
Recently, I've been to France/started playing football, etc. *(note the use of the present perfect here)*
I'm planning to …
After that I'll probably …

I prefer *(followed by a noun)* Scotland because …
I'd rather *(followed by verb)* live in Australia because …

Both my father and mother …
Neither of my brothers …
None of my friends …

It depends. Sometimes I like cooking, and sometimes I'm just too tired.
Definitely, I love it! It's …
Mmm, possibly. It depends on the weather really.
Generally I think it's a good idea because …
Well, it's very different because …

Let me think/see, …
I'm not really sure, but perhaps …
That's a good question/point. I suppose …
I haven't really given that much thought before but …

---

4 Write answers that are true for you to the questions below.

   1 Why are you taking IELTS?
   2 What are your ambitions?
   3 Tell me about where you are living at the moment.
   4 How would you describe your home town?
   5 What do you usually do at the weekend?

Identifying strengths and weaknesses

Remember

- Make sure you answer the question.
- One-word answers are not acceptable.
- Always add some extra information to your answer.

1 ⊙**23** Listen to a student answering the examiner's questions. What is good about their performance? How could it be improved? Use the checklist to help you and refer to the Recording script on page 93.

Checklist

- Does the student answer the questions correctly?
- Does she answer the questions fully, giving extra information?
- Is her grammar accurate?
- Does she use a range of vocabulary appropriately?
- Is it easy to understand her pronunciation?
- Does she use any words or phrases to make her language sound more natural, e.g. *Well, Actually, Oh definitely,* etc?
- Does she sound fluent or does she often hesitate?

---

2 Now record yourself answering the same questions (see page 93 for the questions). Listen to the recording and evaluate your performance using the checklist above.

Planning your answer

In Part 2 of the Speaking module you have to speak for 1–2 minutes on a topic. You have one minute to think about this topic. Use this time well.

1 Read the sample question below. <u>Underline</u> the key words in the instructions.

> Describe an occasion when you have been successful. You should say:
> - where and when you were successful
> - how you were successful
> - what you had to do to make sure you were successful
> and describe how you felt about your success.

2 Think of two or three things to say about each part of the question. You can make notes if you wish, but remember you only have one minute.

Giving extra information

> **Remember**
> It is important to keep talking, but don't talk about things which are not related to the topic.

It is important that you talk for long enough: minimum one minute and maximum two minutes. This means you have to think of extra information to give the examiner. You can do this in different ways by:
- saying why you think/feel something
- giving examples
- giving details

1 Read this sample question and <u>underline</u> the key words.

> Talk about an important day in your life. You should say:
> - when this day was
> - if you were alone or with others
> - where you were and what happened
> and explain why this day was important to you.

2 Think of relevant things to say about each part of the question. Give examples and include details.

3 Use the different parts of the question to organize your answer, so that each part follows on logically from the one before.

4 ⊙24 Now listen to this student answering the question. Does he include all of the main points?

5 Look at the *Useful language* box and practise answering the two sample questions. Time yourself to check your answers are the right length.

> **Useful language**
> The best/worst thing about … is/was …
> The thing I really like(d)/hate(d) about … is/was …
> One of the problems with … is/was …
> I particularly remember … because …
> I'll never forget … because …

1
> Describe a present someone gave you which was/is important to you. You should say:
> - what the present was
> - who gave it to you
> - why they gave it to you (e.g. to celebrate a birthday)
> and explain why it is so important to you.

2
> Describe a friend who has played an important part in your life. You should say:
> - how you met this person
> - how long you have known them
> - the kind of things you do or did with them
> and explain why they have been important in your life.

Identifying strengths and weaknesses

🔘 **25** Listen to two sample answers to Question 2 in exercise 5 above. Do they include all the points in the instruction? Which one is a better answer? Why?

Follow-up questions

After you have spoken for 1–2 minutes, the examiner may ask you one or two follow-up questions about what you have said. For example:

Question	Answer	Follow-up question
How did you feel when you arrived in the UK?	I was very nervous because I didn't know anybody.	Did you find it easy to meet people?

1 Match the appropriate answers **A–F** to questions **1–6**.

  1 Do you enjoy playing sports?
  2 Would you like to go there again?
  3 Do you think it will be easy to get a job in IT?
  4 Have you ever been to any other countries in Europe?
  5 Would you consider doing the same sort of job again?
  6 Would you recommend the holiday to other people?

  A No, not really. It wasn't very good value for money.
  B I don't think so. It wasn't really for me.
  C I expect so. It's a growing industry.
  D Yes, definitely. I particularly enjoy outdoor ones.
  E Possibly. It would depend on who I went with!
  F Yes, a few. France, Spain and the Czech Republic.

2 🔘 **26** Listen and check.

3 🔘 **26** Listen again and repeat the answers.

Part 3

Expanding answers

In Part 3 of the Speaking module, you have to discuss questions related to the topic in Part 2 with the examiner. Although this is a discussion, you should do most of the talking. Sometimes the examiner will ask you questions which seem to need a one-word answer. For example:

  1 Is it a good idea to exercise regularly?
  2 Is there more crime these days?
  3 Do you think children should have mobile phones?

Remember
- One-word answers are not acceptable.
- Always give a reason for your answer.

1 Read the example questions above again. Write an answer for each including a reason.

2 Now add an extra sentence or two to each of your answers.

Linking ideas

1 The words and phrases in the box are all used to link ideas. Put them into the appropriate categories below.

> on the other hand   and   so   because   however   such as

1 the reason for something
2 the result of something
3 joining two ideas together
4 contrasting two ideas
5 giving an example

2 Look at the *Useful language* boxes and practise giving answers to questions **1–8** below.

Useful language: Comparing and contrasting

On the one hand … on the other hand …
Well, … isn't as … as …
… is nowhere near as … as …
I'd rather …
I'd much prefer (to) …
It depends (on) …

Useful language: Making predictions/talking about the future

There's a good chance that …
I doubt very much if …
I hope that …
I expect that …
I'm afraid that … *(this does not mean you feel fear, but is a way of talking about something negative, e.g. I'm afraid that a lot of smokers will complain, but …)*
It's bound to *(+ infinitive)*
It is/isn't very likely to …

Useful language: Giving opinions

As far as I'm concerned …
It seems to me that …
I can't help thinking that … *(use this phrase when you think that people won't agree with you)*
I tend to think that …
I strongly believe that …

---

1 Do you think it's important for young people to spend time with older people?
2 Do you think children should learn financial planning at school or at home?
3 Can you think of some of the negative effects of text messaging?
4 Which is better: living in the countryside or in the city?
5 To what extent are qualifications important?
6 How likely is it that computers will be able to replace humans in the workplace?
7 Would you prefer to watch sport or play it?
8 How do you think global warming will affect transport in the future?

3 ⊙27 Now listen to students answering the eight questions above.
- Do they give full answers?
- Do they use a range of vocabulary?
- Are their answers grammatically correct?

Section 1   Questions 1–10

◎ 28 **Questions 1 and 2**

Circle the appropriate letter.

1   What kind of car does the woman want to rent?
   A   small
   B   two door
   C   manual
   D   automatic

2   When does she want the car?
   A   from Friday to Monday
   B   for the weekend
   C   for four days
   D   next week

Questions 3–6

Complete the notes. Write **NO MORE THAN THREE WORDS OR A NUMBER** for each answer.

Cost of rental (3) £ ...7?...................

Child seat (4) ......no............... cost

(5) ...without rental £500

(6) ...No. of drivers. 2

Question 7

Circle the appropriate letter.

7   How old are Sarah and her husband?
   A   25
   B   under 25
   C   over 25

Questions 8–10

Complete the notes.

Type of car:	Focus
Name of client:	Sarah Middleton
Address:	15 (8) Drysdale Avenue
Collect at:	(9) 8am
Contact phone number:	(10) 079135 7629

Section 2 Questions 11–20

⊙ 29 **Questions 11–15**

Complete the summary. Write **NO MORE THAN THREE WORDS OR A NUMBER** for each answer.

Introduction to the Sports Centre

Sports Centre is open from **(11)** ....7~~ 9pm...... all week. There is a
(12) ...fully equipped room... with exercise machines and **(13)** ...weight-lifting... equipment.
All the equipment has **(14)** ...head-phone connection... so you can listen to music while you get fit
and there are **(15)** ...trainers......... on hand to give you advice and guidance on using the
equipment.

Questions 16–18

Circle the appropriate letters **A**, **B**, **C** or **D**.

16 At the sports centre you can do
    A ballroom dancing.
    B kung fu.
    C circuit training.
    D boxing.

17 Sports centre facilities include
    A a swimming pool.
    B a rugby field.
    C squash courts.
    D indoor running track.

18 Which of the following work at the sports centre?
    A a golf professional
    B fitness instructors
    C tennis coaches
    D football trainers

Questions 19 and 20

Complete the sentences. Write **NO MORE THAN THREE WORDS** for each answer.

19 Off peak members have .... to the Sports Centre.
20 You can pay for your membership online with a ....

Section 3   Questions 21–30

⊙ 30 **Questions 21–24**

Answer the questions. Write **NO MORE THAN THREE WORDS** for each answer.

21 What subject is Andrew studying? ....

22 What is his essay about? ....

23 What is he going to discuss first? ....

24 Which countries are involved most in illegal trade? ....

Questions 25–27

Complete the labels on the diagram:

Participants in transnational human trafficking

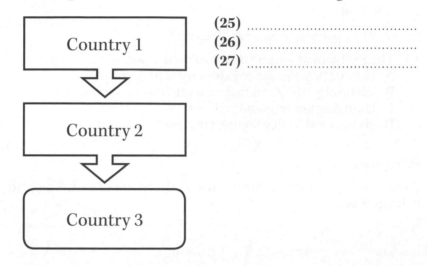

(25) ....
(26) ....
(27) ....

Questions 28–30

Complete the summary. Write **NO MORE THAN THREE WORDS** for each answer.

As well as its involvement in human trafficking, organized crime is responsible for **(28)** .... rare animals. United Nations research has concluded that the solution to international organized crime is not only to prosecute criminals at a **(29)** .... but to cooperate internationally to change **(30)** ....

Section 4   Questions 31–40

⊙ 31 **Questions 31–35**

Complete the sentences. Write **NO MORE THAN THREE WORDS OR A NUMBER** for each answer.

31 The speaker is going to discuss .... because many people think it's a waste of money.

32 Research into space travel has produced advances in ...., such as ultrasound technology.

33 In public health .... have improved the living standards of millions of people.

34 Memory foam was developed to make the seats in .... more comfortable.

35 Research into insulation for space craft has improved .... materials to protect firefighters.

Questions 36–39

Complete the table. Write **NO MORE THAN THREE WORDS OR A NUMBER** for each answer.

Arguments for space exploration	Arguments against space exploration
More accurate prediction of (36) .... improves disaster management planning. (37) Advances in .... systems have made flying safer.	We have not finished (38) .... Earth yet. (39) .... is a more urgent problem and should be given priority.

Question 40

Circle the appropriate letter **A**, **B**, **C** or **D**.

40 The problem of famine could be solved permanently by
   A eliminating the space exploration programme.
   B spending money on research into crop growing.
   C changing government policies.
   D giving food to developing countries.

Reading

Reading Passage 1

You should spend about 20 minutes on **Questions 1–12**, which are based on Reading Passage 1 below.

On 21 May 1932 Los Angeles radio station KHJ transmitted a segment of a motion picture as a television signal for five minutes to a Western Air Express transport plane nearly ten miles away. The experiment was part of a proposed plan to transmit weather information to planes using the emergent technology of television. In this early application of in-flight screened entertainment, the visual communication technology was intended to further the efficiency of transportation technologies. Without accurate weather reports, goods (including human labor) could not be delivered safely and in a timely manner. However, if the experiment was simply to be used as a weather information system, it is unclear why Western Air Express and KHJ broadcast a feature-length film to test the technology. This convergence of entertainment and aviation technologies was a telling indication of a growing alliance between Hollywood and commercial air travel. Although the film (starring Loretta Young) was broadcast without sound, the engineers told reporters, who constituted the majority of those on the plane, that it would require only a small adjustment to also transmit sound, pointing toward the possibility of entertainment applications.

The experiment demonstrated American technical prowess within the ongoing modern project: to eliminate barriers of physical distance and lay claim to the new kinds of spaces created by this project. The television signals were received on a moving vehicle, occupying the relatively new spatial category of 'airspace' (a term barely twenty years old). As the plane itself defied the normal rules of territorial contiguity, flying over Los Angeles but not being in Los Angeles, the transnational communication apparatus of Hollywood became seemingly ethereal. Hollywood, ever ready to take the spotlight for new advancements in entertainment, now took flight to ensure its dominance over the dispersal of cultural content across new spatial categories – the airspace above the world stage.

The introduction of new screen technologies, such as seatback screens on airplanes, has allowed Hollywood to multiply its exhibition sites and circulate its product into places and spaces it could not previously access. Film's standing as an essential part of contemporary culture depends on the ability of film exhibition technologies to transform places into movie theaters (or approximations thereof). Furthermore, the introduction of these new exhibition technologies opens up additional sources for the film industry's revenue stream. In-flight entertainment exemplifies the film industry's intent to create and reach audiences rather than waiting for audiences to find the industry's product. The film industry uses these new exhibition spaces (from which persons often find themselves unable to exit) to promote, market, and sell product. Film is thus no longer part of a menu of entertainment and leisure but a constant, sometimes distracting background. On many airplanes, films appear on screens unbidden, ready to become the central focus of attention if a passenger chooses to listen in via headphones.

Changes in the field of film studies indicate a growing concern and awareness of this multiplicity of new cinematic spaces: movies on television, films on computers, portable DVD players, seatback screens in minivans, and handheld digital media players. From the millennium issue of the journal *Screen* to the adoption of the initial 'M' by the Society for Cinema Studies in 2002, the discipline has increasingly recognized that moving image culture is no longer locatable in the movie theater or on the silver screen. This can also be seen in the emergence of PhD programs, such as Moving Image Studies (Georgia State University) and Screen Cultures (Northwestern University) that by their very names proclaim 'film' to be a limited and perhaps

obsolete demarcation of the presence of moving pictures in contemporary culture. Alongside this effort to find motion pictures in myriad nontheatrical places (a kind of 'ambient cinema,' to paraphrase Anna McCarthy) is a turn toward 'convergence culture' (to borrow from Henry Jenkins), in which motion pictures are seen as but one choice in a menu of digital entertainment options, a single facet of a franchised and remediated property – or merely a piece of intellectual property that converges with other cultural commodities in a single piece of technology. Add to that numerous claims regarding the 'end of cinema,' the death of celluloid, and the downfall of the movie theater, and it becomes an understatement to say there is an ongoing debate over the definition of cinema, the places it occupies, and the spaces it creates.

In-flight entertainment constitutes an apt case study for exploring the issues – screens, convergence, remediation, and the end of cinema – that inform these debates. The practices of in-flight entertainment give rise to useful and productive understandings of trends in media technologies and provide a convenient snapshot of reconfigured spatial relations brought about by networks of rapid communication and rapid transportation technologies. In-flight entertainment offers insight into the globalization of media products. It constitutes yet another venue for film culture, exemplifying the fashion in which film finds an audience (rather than the other way around).

Questions 1–5

Complete the summary below with words from the box. You do not need to use all the words.

| transmission | forecast | experimental | entertainment | weather | radio | sound |
| cinema | moving image |

The first **(1)** .... television broadcast to an aircraft took place in 1932. The original purpose of the **(2)** .... was to see if it was possible to send information about the **(3)** .... to a plane in flight. There was no **(4)** .... on the film that was broadcast. But it was clearly the beginning of in-flight **(5)** ....

Questions 6–10

Do the following statements agree with the information given in Reading Passage 1?
Write:

YES if the statement agrees with the information
NO if the statement contradicts the information
NOT GIVEN if there is no information on this

6 Hollywood was keen to take advantage of the chance to expand into in-flight entertainment. ....

7 The movie industry has been able to increase its income as a result of new technology. ....

8 The latest Hollywood films are shown on transnational flights. ....

9 The film industry is reluctant to seek out new audiences. ....

10 In-flight films are simply a form of entertainment. ....

Questions 11 and 12

Circle the appropriate letters **A**, **B**, **C** or **D**.

11 According to the writer, the discipline of film studies has changed
  A to bring about the death of the cinema.
  B since 2002.
  C to reflect recent trends in the development of multimedia devices.
  D to promote in-flight entertainment.

12 A suitable title for this passage would be:
  A Film studies and the cinema
  B Early experiments in TV transmission
  C The end of Hollywood
  D In-flight entertainment and the globalization of the media

Reading Passage 2

You should spend about 20 minutes on **Questions 13–25**, which are based on Reading Passage 2 below.

A When does a word become a word? For the staff of the *Oxford English Dictionary* it is not a philosophical question, but a practical one. Words are space, time and money. 'What you have to remember,' says Fiona McPherson, senior editor of the *OED*'s new words group, 'is that once a word has gone into the dictionary, it never comes out. So words have to pass a few basic tests before they can be deemed to have entered the language. They have to have been around a reasonable amount of time and be in common use.'

B First published in 1928, after a gestation period of more than fifty years, the *OED* is authoritative, scholarly, but never complete. As soon as the original dictionary was completed, work began on a second edition, published in 1989. A third edition is now in preparation, although it is anybody's guess when it will see the light of day.

C 'The internet has made our work both easier and harder,' says McPherson. 'Being able to store words electronically is a godsend. On the other hand, there are so many potential outlets for new words that it is far more difficult to keep track of changes in the language. 'Since 2000, the twenty-volume *OED* has been available online, with new words added four times a year. There are currently more than 300,000 main entries, and the figure is rising all the time. But coining a clever new word is not enough to make the grade.

D Take 'staycation', a newish word for a holiday taken at home. You see it all the time in newspapers, but it has yet to earn admittance to the *OED*. McPherson and her team want to know that it has the necessary staying power. 'A lot of made-up, punning words of that type have quite a short shelf-life,' she explains. 'In fact, although most people assume 'staycation' first saw the light of day quite recently, I have come across an example of it used by a vicar in the Sixties, to describe people staying away from church.' For the moment, then, it must bide its time, gathering dust in a filing cabinet – one of dozens crammed into a room in Oxford no bigger than a squash court.

E In the internet age, there is something reassuringly human about the process. Open one of the filing cabinets, browse through the dog-eared cards, and you catch the authentic flavour of people who care about words arguing with other people who also care about words. Given the sheer number of new words in circulation, McPherson heads quite a small team: seven full-time staff in Oxford and two in New York, focusing on new American words. But she is not short of reinforcements. A dozen part-time readers scour books,

newspapers and magazines for possible entries to the dictionary. Then there are the volunteers, in their thousands, who write to the *OED* with suggestions.

F A work of high scholarship has always, paradoxically, been the people's dictionary. Sir James Murray, the most famous of all *OED* editors, edited the dictionary from 1879 until his death in 1915, taking personal responsibility for all words beginning with A–D, H–K, O–P and T. However, he was also helped by letters pouring in to Oxford from across the English-speaking world – to the point that a special postbox had to be built outside his house.

G That spirit of democracy is still evident at the *OED* today. A word of Australian origin is as valid as one of Scottish origin; a quotation from *The Sun* as important as one from *The Economist*. The origins of words are as important as their meanings. It may have been Homer Simpson who popularized 'Doh!', now featured in the *OED*, but the word is of much older origin. 'We came across it in a script of *ITMA*, the World War II radio show,' says McPherson.

H For McPherson, the beauty of her work is that it is never done. 'If nobody coined another new word for the next five years, we would still have our hands full,' she says.

Question 13

Circle the appropriate letter **A**, **B**, **C** or **D**.

13 According to Fiona McPherson, words
  A have a practical function.
  B can be taken out of the dictionary.
  C must be used widely.
  D can easily be added to the dictionary.

Questions 14–16

Complete the table below.

Choose **NO MORE THAN THREE WORDS** from the passage for each answer.

Year	Event
1879	Work began on the *OED*
1928	**(14)** ....
1989	**(15)** ....
2000	**(16)** ....

Questions 17–19

Complete the summary of paragraph **C** with words from Reading Passage 2. Write **NO MORE THAN THREE WORDS OR A NUMBER** for each answer.

With the development of the internet it has become easier to
(17) .... but more difficult to follow developments in the
language because the number of **(18)** .... for innovative
vocabulary has increased. To date the Oxford dictionary contains over
(19) .... main words.

Questions 20–22

Look at the following items (Questions 20–22) and the list of groups below. Match each item with the group of people who contribute to the *OED*. Write the correct letter **A–E**.

NB You may use any letter more than once.

20	work in Oxford	....
21	search for new words in printed text	....
22	send in their own ideas	....

A scholars in linguistics
B part-time readers
C volunteers
D full-time *OED* staff
E writers

Questions 23–25

Passage 2 has eight paragraphs, **A–H**.

Choose the correct heading for paragraphs **E–G** from the list of headings below.

23	Paragraph E	....
24	Paragraph F	....
25	Paragraph G	....

> **List of headings**
> **i** Qualifying for the *OED*
> **ii** Staff who work on the *OED*
> **iii** The origins of words
> **iv** The English-speaking world
> **v** Scottish words in the dictionary
> **vi** People who contribute to the *OED*
> **vii** The internet and the *OED*
> **viii** The best known editor of the *OED*

Reading Passage 3

You should spend about 20 minutes on **Questions 26–40**, which are based on Reading Passage 3 below.

A Pupils at a leading public school are to receive weekly 40-minute classes in meditation and stress relief in a ground-breaking addition to the school curriculum.

B Schoolboys aged 14 and 15 at Tonbridge School, in Tonbridge, Kent, were given their first lesson yesterday as part of a course designed with psychologists from the universities of Oxford and Cambridge.

C The project – the first to introduce meditation skills as a regular subject on the curriculum – has been designed specifically for adolescents and comes after the success of a pilot study at the school last year.

D The 'mindfulness' course for Year 10 pupils will last eight weeks. It is designed to develop skills in concentration and to combat anxiety, showing teenagers the benefits of silence and helping them to identify and escape corrosive mindsets that could lead to mental health problems such as depression, eating disorders and addiction.

E The course develops other exercises to help to improve attention – rather than allowing the mind to be 'hijacked' by emotional issues, regrets, worries about the past and future and other distractions. This can be done in a number of ways such as by focusing on breathing, parts of the body or movement.

F Mindfulness originated in Eastern meditation traditions such as Buddhism but is now an established secular discipline. A growing body of research supports wider use of the approach to address transient stress and deeper mental health problems, including recommendations from the National Institute for Health and Clinical Excellence that it be offered on the NHS to patients suffering from depression.

G The project is a collaboration with staff at Charterhouse and Hampton schools – with both institutions planning similar schemes – as well as the Mindfulness Centre at Oxford and the Wellbeing Institute at Cambridge.

Richard Burnett, a divinity teacher and housemaster at Tonbridge who is leading the course, told *The Times* that the lessons demanded a 'culture change' in the perceptions of silence for teachers and pupils.

'One of the things about schools is that silence is associated with power – the teacher tells the pupils to be quiet. What you need to do is convey the idea that silence is a positive activity to be savoured and enjoyed,' he said.

He said that while some children involved in the trial had been sceptical, most had embraced the challenge that it posed in the classroom. The pupils said that they hoped to use the mindfulness in the future to help to battle anxieties and to put things in perspective. They also said that they found it helpful for getting to sleep and becoming less nervous about school cricket matches.

Mark Williams, director of the Mindfulness Centre at Oxford, said that Tonbridge was the first school to introduce a full meditation course in a practical rather than academic context. Professor Williams said: 'This is not about converting people to Buddhism, but showing there is scientific evidence that these practices are useful. So why deny them from being used?' In March, Tonbridge is to host a conference, with Professor Williams as a speaker, that aims to encourage mindfulness uptake in schools.

Andrew McCulloch, chief executive of the Mental Health Foundation, said mindfulness training also offered the chance to take proactive steps to avoid depression and anxiety in later life.

'These problems have their roots in early life, so if you can learn techniques when you are young you might never have a breakdown,' he said.

Staying focused

The first lesson, being run this week, is described as 'puppy training' – comparing the mind with a puppy that needs to learn how to 'stay' and focus on one thing, rather than running around in a distracted fashion.

Other stages of the course include: establishing calm and concentration; recognising rumination; developing present-moment awareness in the everyday; slowing and savouring activities; stepping back from thoughts that hijack you; allowing, accepting and being with difficult emotions; reflection and making it personal.

It uses figures from popular culture to help to explain the benefits of mindfulness, including rugby player Jonny Wilkinson, who uses meditation techniques to help his concentration when kicking for goal, and Po, a lethargic panda who transforms his attitude in the DreamWorks' film *Kung Fu Panda*.

Each class has one 40-minute lesson a week, with a weekly MP3 file of mindfulness exercises that pupils are encouraged to listen to before evening homework.

Questions 26–29

Look at paragraphs **A–G** in Reading Passage 3. Which paragraphs focus on the following information?

NB Only write **ONE** letter for each answer.

Example

Details of changes in the programme of studies in a secondary school. **A**

26 The purpose of the course ....
27 The effects of mindfulness ....
28 Who the course is for ....
29 How the course achieves its aims ....

Questions 30–32

Complete each sentence with the correct ending **A–F** from the box below.

NB You may use any letter more than once.

30 One of the aims of the course was to change ...
31 Mindfulness is not only useful in the classroom but can be used to ...
32 The course is based on ...

> **A** the personal experience of the director of the Mindfulness Centre.
> **B** win cricket matches more easily.
> **C** scientific proof that it is effective.
> **D** the concept of silence in the classroom.
> **E** perceptions of power.
> **F** overcome stress and fear.

Questions 33–36

Do the following statements agree with the information given in Reading Passage 3?
Write:

YES   if the statement agrees with the information given
NO   if the statement contradicts the information given
NOT GIVEN if there is no information about this

33 The course in meditation at Tonbridge is designed by psychiatrists. ....
34 Mindfulness originated in India. ....
35 Mental problems usually start in childhood. ....
36 Jonny Wilkinson uses mindfulness to improve his concentration. ....

Questions 37–40

Complete the summary. Choose your answers from the box.

NB There are more answers than spaces so you do not need to use them all.

concentration	thinking	calmer	intelligent	lethargic	optimism	anxiety
body	kindness	mindfulness	negative	attitude	exercise	

Through the practice of **(37)** .... it is possible to control your thoughts and improve your levels of **(38)** .... This will help you to become **(39)** .... and reduce your feelings of **(40)** .... As a result you may learn to be more efficient.

Writing Task 1

You should spend about 20 minutes on this task.

The graph below shows leisure activities by age in England in 2007 and 2008.

Summarize the information by selecting and reporting the main features, and make comparisons where relevant.

You should write at least 150 words.

Selected activities performed in free time: by age, 2007/08 England

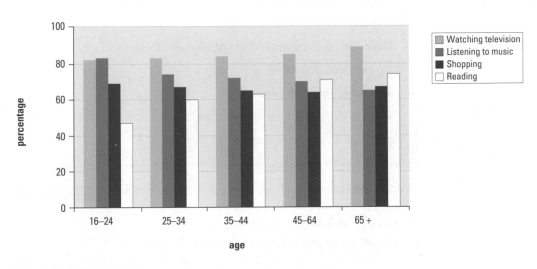

Writing Task 2

You should spend about 40 minutes on this task.

We should always take environmental factors into consideration when we buy consumer goods. To what extent do you agree or disagree with this statement?

You should write at least 250 words.

Use your own ideas, knowledge and experience and support your arguments with examples and relevant evidence.

Part 1

The examiner asks you some general questions about yourself, your home, your job or your studies. For example:

- Where are you living at the moment?
- What are the best things about your home town?
- Why did you choose to study [..]?
- What do you like about your job?

Part 2

The examiner gives you a card with questions similar to those below. You have one minute to think about the topic and make notes if you wish. You should then talk about the topic for 1–2 minutes.

> Describe an old person that you admire. You should say:
>
> - who this person is
> - where you met them
> - how long you have known them
>
> and explain why you admire this person.

When you have finished, the examiner asks a few brief questions about what you have said. For example:
- Do you still see this person?
- Do other people admire them, too?

Part 3

The examiner will ask some discussion questions related to the same topic. For example:
- What do you think young people can learn from older people?
- Do you think young people respect old people as much as they did in the past?
- What do you think older people have to contribute to the community?
- Do you think there should be a compulsory retirement age?
- How do you think society should be dealing with the problem of an increasingly aging population?

Answer key

Key for Listening module

Quiz p. 7

1. **B** The Listening module is about 40 minutes long – 30 minutes of listening and 10 minutes at the end to transfer your answers to the answer sheet.
2. **A** There are four sections.
3. **C** There are 40 questions which may include multiple choice, short answers, filling in charts/diagrams/tables, sentence completion, matching and classifying.
4. True. The texts and questions get more difficult with each section.
5. True. All the sections are worth the same number of marks, even though the exam gets more difficult.
6. Adam ... **C**   1 **C**
   Professor Jones ... **A**   2 **B**
   Steve, Mary and Sarah ... **D** 3 **D**
   Mr Green ... **B**   4 **A**
7. Once.
8. Yes. Before each section, you have about 30 seconds to read the questions for that section.
9. On the question paper, and then transfer them at the end to the answer sheet.
10. True.

Prediction p. 7

1 a a girl (a new student) and another person (Q.1)
   b the girl (Q.3)
   c at college (Q.1)
   d directions (Q.2 and Q.3)
   e go to the accommodation office (Q.3)

2 1 **A:** 'I only arrived here yesterday'
   2 **C:** 'The one with the glass front.'
   3 **C:** '... and it's the second door on the left?'

Recognizing repetition and avoiding distracters p. 8

1 Keiko repeats the directions back to Stephan for confirmation.

2 In the last extract, Stephan replied 'That's right!' He means, 'You are correct', but if you are not listening carefully, you might think that the <u>door</u> is on the right.

Completing notes p. 8

1 1 think carefully
   2 near (to) home
   3 study overseas/abroad

3 and 4

1 *£130:* 'That's £130 per week, or £90 without meals.' £90 is incorrect because this is the price without meals.
2 *college halls/halls of residence/college residential block:* 'There are three kinds of accommodation that we deal with – home stays, college halls of residence, or private lets.' The instructions do not state that you should use

words from the text, so you can use your own, and in this case, you have to as *college halls of residence* is four words and would be incorrect. *College halls residence* is also incorrect as it is ungrammatical.
3 *reasonably priced/fairly priced:* '... but we make sure that you are paying a reasonable price.' You need to change the words from the text to make grammatical sense.

5 4 Jenkins
   5 British
   6 562 Green Park Road
   7 07785 265981

Listening for numbers and letters p. 9

3
   1 forward slash
   2 hyphen
   3 colon
   4 semi-colon
   5 dot

4
1 *Sir Anthony Winton.* Make sure you can spell *Mr, Mrs, Miss, Ms* and *Sir.*
2 *34.92.* Numbers after the decimal point are always said individually, e.g. *point nine two*, not *point ninety-two.*
3 *15 Sparrow Lane.* Make sure you can spell words like *Lane.*
4 *29,030* (feet)
5 *Michael MacWilliams.* There is another capital letter after *Mc* or *Mac.*
6 *286 Banbury Road.* Abbreviations for *road* (Rd) and *street* (St) are acceptable.
7 *74%*
8 *Janet Gates*
9 *0121 674 9544.* All numbers are said separately, except for *double 4*, and there is a pause between each set of numbers.
10 *654/120084* (/ is usually pronounced *forward slash*)
11 *Mrs J Robson-Smith.* If someone has two surnames, there is a hyphen between them.
12 *Flat 3, 547 Oxford Road*
13 *www.bht.co.uk* (. is pronounced *dot* in web addresses)
14 *Dr Brown*
15 *N770 CES.* Numbers are pronounced separately for ID/registration numbers.

Skills practice p. 10

1 D
2 B
3 set menu/three-course meal
4 vegetarian/made without meat
5 coffee/cappuccino or espresso
6 12
7 25
8 (Mr) (Dan) Glover
9 01452 863092

Using key words for prediction p. 11

1 1 **A** <u>used car sales</u> (e.g. second-hand cars)
  B <u>the best way to buy a car</u> (e.g. most efficient/most effective)
  C <u>the most popular way to sell a car</u> (Note that this is talking about selling, while the others mention buying a car.)
  D <u>different ways of buying a new car</u> (This answer is the only one that specifies new cars.)

 2 **A** <u>new driver</u> (e.g. you have just passed your test)
  B <u>accident</u> (Listen for words like *crash* or *smash*.)
  C <u>too old to be repaired</u>. (Listen for *the end/not worth repairing*.)
  D <u>not in a hurry</u> (Listen for opposites like *desperate/to get out*)

 3 **A** <u>a lot of room</u> (e.g. there is a lot of space)
  B <u>cheap</u> (or *inexpensive*)
  C <u>legal right to return the car</u> (e.g. a warranty/guarantee)
  D <u>honest</u> (e.g. they are trustworthy/they won't cheat you)

2
 1 A
 2 A and C
 3 C

Eliminating wrong answers p. 11

3 1 **A** CORRECT. 'Today we're going to talk about the different ways there are of buying a used car ...'
  B INCORRECT. Not 'the best way' but 'the different ways' of buying a car.
  C INCORRECT. The recording specifies 'of *buying* a used car.'
  D INCORRECT. The recording talks about used cars, not new cars.

 2 **A** CORRECT. The recording says, '... maybe you've just passed your test ...'
  B INCORRECT. Nothing is mentioned about an accident.
  C CORRECT. The recording says, '... your old car has broken down again ... this really is the end for it and it's not worth repairing ...'
  D INCORRECT. The recording says '... and are desperate to get out on the road'. This means you want to drive very much.

Note: with this type of question, if you choose fewer answers than you are asked for, even if they are correct you will <u>not</u> get <u>any</u> marks.

 3 **A** INCORRECT. The place where cars are sold is called a *showroom*.
  B INCORRECT. Dealers are usually about £800–£1,000 more expensive.
  C CORRECT. If something goes wrong with the car after you've bought it, you can take it back.
  D INCORRECT. This isn't mentioned.

Completing a summary p. 11

1 1 This must be an adjective such as *good/better/safe(r)/cheap(er)* and the context suggests that it is a positive adjective.
 2 This must be a noun: what kind of things can you look through?
 3 The article tells us that this must be a noun and relates to 'warranty'.

 4 The answer to this is probably a person or a time and might be followed by a preposition (e.g. *check out/check over*).
 5 This must be a noun: what will you not have at an auction?

2
Note: there is often more than one acceptable answer to these questions, because the question doesn't state that you have to use words from the text.
 1 *cheaper/less expensive* 'If you're looking for a cheaper car ...'
 2 *(local) papers/adverts* '... by looking in the adverts in your local paper.'
 3 *(obvious) problem/disadvantage/difficulty* 'The obvious problem is that once you've bought the car it's yours and you can't really take it back.'
 4 *over/by a mechanic/before you buy* '... get a mechanic to check it over for you before you buy it.'
 5 *time* '... you won't really have time to check the car over.'

Skills practice p. 12

 1 B
 2 C
 3 C
 4 A
 5 travel insurance
 6 (quite) expensive
 7 too much sun/the sun
 8 clean your teeth/have *or* use ice
 9 liquid(s)/bottled water/soft drinks/fruit juice

Listening for specific speakers p. 13

 1 There are three speakers. They greet each other by name.
 2 Robert, Anand and Claire.
 3 Robert and Claire speak twice. Anand speaks three times.

Listening for specific information/short answers p. 13

1
The answer to Question 2 must be a number because it asks 'What is the <u>word limit</u> for the assignment?'

The answer to Question 3 must be a location or a situation: where might you get an idea? '<u>Where</u> did Robert get his idea for a topic from?'

Recent ecological problems will be students' own answers but examples might include melting polar ice or ozone depletion.

2 1 **A** *water pollution*
  B *global warming*
   'Oh, you know, <u>water pollution</u> like the oil tanker that broke up and killed all the sea life for miles near Spain, or the kind of thing that's always talked about, like <u>global warming</u>.'

 2 *2,000 words*
  Robert: What's the <u>word limit</u>, again? Is it 1,500 words, as usual?
  Anand: No, this one's 500 words longer.
  Claire: <u>2,000</u>? Help! We've got more work than I thought!

 3 *an internet search/the internet*. 'Have you got any <u>ideas for a topic</u>?' 'I looked through books in the library and some journals, but what worked in the end was <u>an internet search</u>.'

Completing a table p. 13

1 Questions 1 and 4 ask you to identify the types of pollution. Question 2 must be a date.

2

Pollution problem	Solution provided by	Date completed
(1) *Sewage*	City Council	**(2)** *1970s*
Boat traffic	**(3)** *State government*	next year
(4) *Rubbish*	**(5)** *(Local) divers/diving clubs*	ongoing project

Matching p. 14

1

How do each of the following relate to the <u>problem</u> of <u>pollution</u> in the <u>harbour</u>?

2 1 **C**
   2 **A**
   3 **B**
   4 **B**

Spelling p. 14

1 and 2

1 *site* (NOT *sight*). Take care with words that have more than one meaning and spelling, but which sound the same.
2 *6th February/February 6* (US). The month MUST begin with a capital letter.
3 *Wednesday.* Days of the week MUST begin with a capital letter.
4 *suggest*
5 *inexpensive.* Take care with prefixes.
6 *Unemployment*
7 *advise* (NOT *advice*). Note that the sound is different, and here a verb is needed.
8 *politician* (NOT *polititian*). Take care with *-ian* endings.
9 *companies.* Take care with the plural, especially irregular plurals or those which take *-ies*.
10 *easier.* Remember *easy ends with a 'y', but changes to an 'i' when 'er' is added.*
11 *independent.* Take care with *-ent/-ant* endings.
12 *Receiving.* Take care with the order of *i* and *e*.

3 *constant, perceived* and *sufficient* are spelt wrongly.

Skills practice p. 15

	'A' Levels	Foundation Course
Length of course	2 years	1 year
Number of subjects studied	2–3	**(1)** *1*
English language support given	often none	**(2)** *6 hours* per *week*
Main type of assessment	exam(s)	**(3)** *continuous assessment or assignments and presentations*
Most popular with	**(4)** *British students*	overseas students

5 academic
6 essay structure/essays
7 global markets
8 It sounds hard/difficult.

9 M
10 A
11 M
12 P

Labelling a diagram with numbered parts p. 16

1 1 *Diagram 1:* shows a process. It's a good idea to think about where the process starts and what the most important parts of the process are.
Diagram 2: shows an object. Parts of an object will usually be described in relation to each other, so think about which parts are next to, above or below each other.
Diagram 3: shows a map. For plans, think about which way the plan is orientated, and where features like doors, staircases, etc are. For maps, look for roads, buildings, rivers, etc.

2 **Diagram 1**
  A *light rays.* '... light rays from the object, ... come through the lens ...'
  B *virtual image.* '... sees a virtual image, which is closer and smaller than the real object.'
  Diagram 2
  A *clock face.* '... on the front of the clock, we call this the clock face ...'
  B *pendulum.* '... and behind that, the *pendulum.* That's P-E-N-D-U-L-U-M.'
  C *weight.* '... driven by a weight, which is situated in front of the pendulum ...'
  Diagram 3
  A *cafeteria.* '... and the cafeteria is right behind it. You can get to the cafeteria through the Students' Union, or through a separate entrance at the back.'
  B *(a large) lawn.* 'If you walk out of the main entrance to the Union, there is a large lawn area ...'
  C *library.* '... to your left is the library ...'

3 The diagram shows a hydroelectric plant. A is behind the dam; B is under the ground; C is under the dam; D joins the plant and leads away from it.

4 A *reservoir.* '... a large artificial lake, called a reservoir. That's R-E-S-E-R-V-O-I-R.'
  B *turbine.* 'The turbine is situated underground. Sorry, what was that? Oh, turbine, T-U-R-B-I-N-E.'
  C *control gate.* '... under the dam there is a control gate and this can be opened to let the water in.'
  D *power lines.* '... by the power lines, shown leading away from the power station.'

Labelling a flow chart p. 17

1 Answer 1 must be a number – it's asking for a number of volts.

2 1 100,000
  2 distributes the power
  3 (normal) domestic (electric)
  4 (electrical) accidents/accidents with electricity

Sentence completion p. 17

1 1 You need adjectives to complete these gaps. What kind of positive adjectives could be used about hydroelectricity?
  2 You need a noun here. What kind of factors limit hydroelectricity?

2 1 *clean/green, sustainable* '... it is a very clean and green method ... and it's sustainable ...'

2 *(a large) river/reliable water (flow)* '... obviously a large river is needed with a reliable flow of water ...'

Listening for signpost words p. 17

1 B This phrase is used after the speaker has recapped on previously given information, before the speaker moves on to a new point.

2 B In this context, the speaker is drawing attention to a visual, but this could also be used to emphasize a point.

3 A If this phrase is used, the information that follows is usually related to what went before, but not usually contrasting it.

Skills practice p. 18

1 600 million
2 sediment/sand and mud
3 heat
4 sandstone/limestone (NOT reservoir rock)
5 oil
6 faulting
7 cap rock
8 (access) roads
9 water
10 reserve pit
11 (the) main (drilling) hole
12 brought in

Key for Reading module

Quiz p. 19

1 B
2 C
3 B
4 A, B, C, E (advertisements can be found in the General Training Reading module).
5 False (unlike the Listening module).
6 False (the texts and tasks do not increase in difficulty as the test progresses).
7 False (there are a variety of question types, including multiple choice, short answer questions, completing sentences/notes/charts/diagrams, matching, classifying, etc.).
8 True (although all the topics are of general interest and require no specialist knowledge of the subject matter).

Skimming for gist p. 19

i *Beautiful butterflies.* This is not correct because only paragraph B describes the beauty of butterflies. The rest of the text is not concerned with this.

ii *The life cycle of the butterfly.* This is not correct. Although the text mentions the different stages of the butterfly's life cycle, the focus is on their feeding habits.

iii *Butterflies in decline.* This is correct because the text describes several historical periods when butterflies have been widespread and contrasts them with the current situation when they are threatened by modern farming methods.

iv *Butterflies and farming.* This is not correct because farming is only mentioned in paragraphs E and F.

Matching headings to paragraphs p. 21

ix The beauty of butterflies

B Certainly butterflies are loved partly for their <u>extravagant beauty</u> and the decoration they bring to summer days. Their abstract wing <u>patterns</u> were clearly Modern <u>Art</u> before humans had got round to inventing it.

vii Research into butterflies

C But Henry Walter Bates followed his remark about the frivolity of butterflies with this: 'The <u>study</u> of butterflies ... instead of being despised, will someday be valued as one of the most important <u>branches</u> of <u>Biological science</u>.' That day is coming to pass.

iv Contamination and living creatures

D In <u>natural ecosystems</u> there are some <u>organisms</u> that are more sensitive to change than others: they are the <u>canaries</u> in the coalmine, <u>harbingers</u>. <u>Lichens</u> are often cited as early warning indicators of <u>pollution</u>, but although rather gorgeous in their way, if they disappeared their absence would not be felt as keenly as that of the <u>butterflies</u>.

ii Butterflies' susceptibility to changes in nature

E <u>Butterflies</u> are <u>ecologically vulnerable</u> because they are <u>specialists</u>. Everyone knows that they love colourful, scented <u>flowers</u> rich in nectar, but in their <u>larval phase</u> – the <u>caterpillars</u> – they have <u>stringent requirements</u> for quite different <u>plants</u>. Most <u>caterpillars</u> feed on a <u>very limited range</u> of <u>plants</u>, many on a <u>single species</u>, and it is almost never one of the plants on which the adults feed. Some <u>adult butterflies</u>, in fact, don't feed at all: their sole purpose is to mate and lay eggs. For some species this takes a few days only, and they rely on the energy stores that they are born with (fruit of the caterpillar's munching). Professor David Bellamy, passionate naturalist and conservationist, laments the <u>loss</u> of the <u>butterfly paradise</u> he experienced as a boy growing up during the Second World War, when every bomb site quickly filled with flowers. But butterfly-luring flowers. But it's the bombshell of modern <u>agribusiness</u>, with its <u>monocultures, herbicides and pesticides</u> and hence <u>loss of biodiversity</u>, that he blames for the dramatic <u>declines</u> in many of our native butterflies.

v A countryside suitable for butterflies

F But he reminds us that hard economics and <u>wild nature</u> are not irrevocably at odds. 'We can have our cake and eat it. Because without bees and <u>butterflies</u> what would pollinate our plants?' He paints a vivid picture of the rise and fall of the <u>butterfly-friendly environment</u> in Britain. 'Ten thousand years ago woolly mammoths roamed here in Ice Age conditions. Seven thousand years ago, as the climate warmed, England was mostly <u>forest</u>, and there would have been <u>few butterflies</u> in such dense woodland. It was Neolithic <u>farmers</u> and their successors who created the <u>patchwork of fields, hedges and copses</u> – a <u>landscape</u> in which butterflies could <u>thrive</u>.'

iii Our responsibility to care for the environment

G For Bellamy, it is this <u>stewardship</u> of the <u>environment</u> that matters. Having created, through traditional agriculture, a landscape that both fed us and fostered biodiversity, we need to return to <u>good husbandry</u>: 'gamekeepers are our best <u>guardians</u>', he says. Bellamy is passionate about reinstating a butterfly-friendly <u>habitat</u> – 'As we made it, we can mend it. It will come back quickly' – and he looks forward to 'the renaissance of the British landscape', quoting Churchill: 'a landscape worth dying for'.

The following choices were not correct:

i *The life cycle of a caterpillar.* Although this is mentioned in paragraph E, the main topic is the vulnerability of butterflies because of their feeding habits.

vi *Modern Art.* Butterflies' wings are compared to Modern Art, but the topic of paragraph B is their beauty.

viii *Contrasting bees and butterflies.* Paragraph A describes the differences and similarities between bees and butterflies.

Labelling diagrams p. 21

Look for numbers and periods in history (like *Second World War*) and words like *ago, decline* and *thrive*.

1 B   2 A   3 D   4 C

Multiple choice p. 22

1 Butterflies are important because
   A INCORRECT because while the statement is true, it is not the reason why they are important.
   B INCORRECT. This is true, but does not make butterflies important. (Paragraph E)
   C CORRECT. Paragraph D refers to lichens as organisms that warn us of the dangers of pollution but comments '... if they [lichens] disappeared their absence would not be felt as keenly as that of the butterflies.'
   D INCORRECT because this is not mentioned in the text.

2 Pollution affects butterflies in particular because
   A CORRECT. Butterflies are ecologically vulnerable because they are specialists. (Paragraph E)
   B INCORRECT. This is true but not relevant to the effects of pollution.
   C INCORRECT. This is true but not relevant to the effects of pollution.
   D INCORRECT. This is not true.

3 The cause of the decline of the butterfly population is
   A INCORRECT. The text says, '... during the Second World War, when every bomb site quickly filled with flowers. But butterfly-luring flowers.' (Paragraph E)
   B CORRECT. But it's the bombshell of modern agribusiness, with its monocultures, herbicides and pesticides and hence loss of biodiversity, that he blames for the dramatic declines in many of our native butterflies. (Paragraph E)
   C INCORRECT. The opposite is true. (Paragraph E)
   D INCORRECT. The opposite is true. (Paragraph F)

4 Butterflies were plentiful when
   A INCORRECT because butterflies need flowers to survive.
   B INCORRECT. '... there would have been few butterflies in such dense woodland.' (Paragraph F)
   C CORRECT. 'It was Neolithic farmers and their successors who created the patchwork of fields, hedges and copses – a landscape in which butterflies could thrive.' (Paragraph F)
   D INCORRECT. 'But it's the bombshell of modern agribusiness, with its monocultures, herbicides and pesticides and hence loss of biodiversity, that he blames for the dramatic declines in many of our native butterflies.' (Paragraph E)
   E CORRECT. '... every bomb site quickly filled with flowers. But butterfly-luring flowers.'

5 Caterpillars and butterflies eat
   A INCORRECT. This is not mentioned.
   B INCORRECT. 'Most caterpillars feed on a very limited range of plants ...' (Paragraph E)
   C INCORRECT. Only certain species of adult butterflies do not feed at all. (Paragraph E)
   D CORRECT. '... and it is almost never one of the plants on which the adults feed.' (Paragraph E)
   E INCORRECT. They feed on '... a limited range of plants ...'
   F CORRECT. '... they love colourful, scented flowers rich in nectar ...' (Paragraph E)
   G CORRECT. '... they are specialists.' (Paragraph E)

Guessing meaning from context p. 22

1 *Native* butterflies are in decline. *'Native'* is an adjective in this example. But it can also be a noun, e.g. *He's a native of Birmingham*, which means he was born in Birmingham.

2 *butterfly-luring* is an adjective. It describes the type of flowers.

2 *stewardship:* husbandry; *environment:* landscape, habitat; *created:* made

Skills practice p. 23

1 iii Carbon footprint labelling
2 B vi
3 C iii
4 D ii
5 orange juice
6 wholemeal bread
7 meat/beef
8 1 kg
9 A
10 C
11 D
12 milk
13 crisps
14 Coca-Cola®
15 C
16 B
17 C

Skimming for gist p. 26

C

Scanning to find information quickly p. 26

1 1 B
   2 C
   3 D

Short answer questions p. 28

1 Paragraph D – Many new coal-fired power plants are expected to capture CO_2 emissions and store it safely underground, rather than pump it into the atmosphere. Plants increasingly will turn coal into a gas, rather than burn it. They will then burn the gas to generate power, or use it as raw material for a variety of chemical products, while CO_2 will be captured and stored.

2 Paragraph E – So, while the world races to build up alternative fuels, it must also find new sources of fossil fuels, including unconventional ones, such as oil sands. And we must accelerate efforts to make fossil fuels

cleaner, <u>by reducing the CO_2 emitted in their production and use</u>.

3 Paragraph F – Billions more must go into <u>upgrading electricity transmission networks</u> to handle increased demand and the on-and-off power generated by wind and solar.

Understanding paraphrasing p. 29

A paraphrase may look similar in meaning, but be careful to look out for words like *all, every, no*, etc. These can change the meaning.

1 If governments adopt the right <u>rules and incentives</u>, by the <u>middle of this century renewable sources</u> will provide <u>nearly 30 per cent</u> of the world's energy.	***Same*** *By implementing <u>effective policies</u>, governments can ensure that <u>almost a third</u> of energy production will come from <u>alternative sources</u> by 2050.*
2 Greater variety of fuel choices will be a boon for consumers. Different fuels will be stronger in different regions.	***Different*** *'The <u>range of available fuels will expand</u> ...' does not include the idea that customers will benefit from this.*
3 <u>Wind, solar and hydropower</u> will account for <u>30 per cent of electricity generation by 2030</u>, up from <u>about 18 per cent</u> today.	***Same*** *By the <u>third decade of the 21st century</u>, sustainable energy sources will generate <u>a third of our electricity</u>, an increase of 12 per cent on current figures.*
4 Indeed, <u>fossil fuels; coal, oil and natural gas</u>, will continue to provide <u>more than half</u> the world's energy <u>in 2050</u>, building <u>a long bridge to an era when alternatives can take over</u>.	***Same*** *As <u>the process of converting to alternative energy sources will take a long time, non-renewable fuels</u> will still account for <u>over 50%</u> of our global energy production in the <u>middle of the 21st century</u>.*

True, False or *Not Given* and *Yes, No* or *Not Given* p. 29

1 NO '... by the middle of this century renewable sources will provide nearly 30 per cent of the world's energy.' (Paragraph A) '... fossil fuels; coal, oil and natural gas, will continue to provide more than half the world's energy in 2050, building a long bridge to an era when alternatives can take over.' (Paragraph E)

2 NO '... some of them capable of plugging in to recharge their batteries.' (Paragraph B)

3 YES '... more than double today's total.' (Paragraph B)

4 NOT GIVEN This may be true, but it is not mentioned in the text.

5 YES 'In Brazil, ethanol from sugar cane already supplies more than 40 per cent of demand for petrol.' (Paragraph C)

6 NOT GIVEN Nuclear power is not discussed in the article.

Recognizing opinion p. 29

1 1 O. The speaker makes a prediction, but cannot support it with evidence. 'Society will be on the road toward sustainable mobility. The world's highways will rumble and whir with vehicles powered by all manner of energy ...' (Paragraph A)

2 O. 'Planners at Shell think that by 2020 up to 15 per cent of new cars worldwide could be hybrid electrics ...' (Paragraph B)

3 F. 'In Brazil, ethanol from sugar cane already supplies more than 40 per cent of demand for petrol.' (Paragraph C)

4 F. '... but governments will need to continue using tax credits and other incentives to encourage the growth of renewables.' (Paragraph G)

5 F. '... renewables account for about seven per cent of global energy.' (Paragraph G)

2 1 B (Paragraph E)
2 E (Paragraph B)
3 C (Paragraph B)
4 D (Paragraph A and D) Paragraph A says '... nearly 30 per cent', Paragraph D says '... 30 per cent'

3 2 The author's main focus is on the future development of fuel and energy production.

Skills practice p. 30

1 C
2 B
3 G
4 D
5 climate change (Paragraph B)
6 ¼ – ⅓ (Paragraph C)
7 US$83 billion per year (Paragraph D)
8 China (Paragraph F)
9 FALSE. 'Equally crucial is lower tech research into basics such as crop rotation ...' (Paragraph C)
10 TRUE. '... reinventing farming requires a multidisciplinary approach ...' (Paragraph D)
11 TRUE. '... most resource-limited countries, where the majority of the world's population lives and where population growth over the next decades will be greatest.' (Paragraph D)
12 NOT GIVEN
13 A '... while increasing today's brand of resource-intensive, environmentally destructive agriculture is a poor option.' (Paragraph B)
14 B '... crops that are more resistant to drought, heat, submersion ...' (Paragraph C)
15 C 'In Africa, the lack of roads also hampers agricultural productivity, making it expensive and difficult for farmers to get synthetic fertilizers.' (Paragraph D)
16 A 'The big exceptions are China, where spending has grown exponentially over the past decade, and, to a lesser extent, India and Brazil. (Paragraph F)
17 C 'Recently, however, they have begun to engage in public-private partnerships to generate crops that meet the needs of poorer countries.' (Paragraph G)
18 B 'And research agendas need to be focused on the needs of the poorest and most resource-limited countries ...' (Paragraph D)

Summary completion p. 33

1 international
2 employers
3 minority
4 Half

Guessing meaning from context p. 34

1 and 2

1 enhances – '... *enhances our position in the global economy* ...' (Paragraph A)
2 encourage – '*We would* encourage *people to study abroad because we can see the great benefits* ...' (Paragraph C)
3 impact – '... *so the* impact *they might have on our economy or society* *would be very small*.' (Paragraph E)
4 encroaching – '... *are fast encroaching* on that territory.' (Paragraph F)
5 net – '*We know that the UK is* a net importer *of foreign students* ...' (Paragraph F)
6 outward – '*Outward mobility – the number of* British *students taking places at international universities* ...' (Paragraph G)

Note completion p. 34

1 highest qualifications – '*Interestingly, those with the highest qualifications were the most likely to intend to return to the UK,* ...'
2 migrate – '... *those who were studying abroad in order to migrate – which happens a lot when it comes to studying in Australia* ...'
3 expertise – '... *those who wanted to access particular expertise* ... '

Understanding paraphrasing and sentence completion p. 34

1 1 building broader networks (Paragraph A)
2 limiting yourself to your national borders (Paragraph B)
3 pack their bags and go (Paragraph C)
4 undertaking higher education (Paragraph D)
5 to assess the benefits of international study (Paragraph E)

2 1 B '... planned to return.' (Paragraph G)
2 C '... a number of UK postgraduate science, technology and engineering courses could collapse without international students.' (Paragraph F)
3 D 'It's difficult to assess the benefits of international study to us as a nation, because the numbers going are quite small, ...' (Paragraph E)

3 1 *at international universities* (Paragraph A)
2 *national borders* (Paragraph B)
3 *professional level* (Paragraph C)
4 *reluctant to leave* (Paragraph D)

1 genetics
2 characteristics
3 personality
4 ethical
5 drugs
6 sports
7 Doping
8 rules
9 G
10 D
11 F
12 B
13 Genetic testing
14 guidelines and policies
15 performance-enhancing
16 genetic material

Key for Writing module

Quiz p. 37

1 B
2

	How long should you spend on this task?	Minimum number of words
Task 1	20 minutes	150
Task 2	40 minutes	250

Task 2 carries more marks than Task 1 so don't spend more than twenty minutes on Task 1.
3 B But don't forget that occasionally the question may require you to describe a process.
4 A

Understanding data p. 37

1 1 Figure 2
2 Figure 3
3 Figure 4
4 Figure 1
2 1 D
2 C
3 E
4 F
5 A
6 B
3 1 Figure 4
2 Figure 2
3 Figure 3
4 Figure 1
4 Figure 1   1 contemporary or period drama (4%)
             2 sport (live sport 13% and other sport 8%)
    Figure 2   1 around 30,000
             2 2003
    Figure 3   1 vehicle purchase
             2 2008
    Figure 4   1 1971
             2 people under 16

Language focus: Expressing figures and quantities p. 38

1 1 50 per cent, 10 per cent
2 2002, 2009
3 2007, 2009
4 25 per cent, 2008

2 1 *exactly the same* (6%). A similar expression is *identical*.
2 *twice as many* (8% and 4%) means *two times as many*. Similar expressions include *three or four times as many*.
3 *much more* (from 28,000 to 134,000 compared with 28,500 to 79,000). A similar expression is *much less*. *Far more/less* can be used with adjectives, e.g. *far more expensive* as an alternative to *much more expensive/much cheaper*.
4 *more than trebled* (from 28,000 to 134,000) means it *increased (more than) three times*. Similar expressions include *more than doubled* which means *twice* or *quadrupled* which means *four times*.
5 *slightly more* (21 GBP compared to 18). A similar expression is *slightly less*. These phrases are more appropriate than *a little more/less*.
6 *very little*. Use *little* for uncountable nouns, *few* for countable nouns.
7 *a quarter* (¼) Similar expressions include *a half, three quarters, a third* but do not use complicated fractions, e.g. *three-fifths*. Percentages are also an option.
8 *half as many* (12 compared to 25). Use *many* for countable nouns (*people* in this case), *much* for uncountable nouns.

The opening statement p. 39

1 A This simply uses the same words as the heading for the chart. Remember copying will not gain you any marks.
B The chart does not provide information about ages so it has not been described correctly.
C This sentence provides an accurate description of the general trends shown in the chart without including any statistical data and is therefore the best opening statement.
D The data has not been interpreted correctly (the number of first marriages did not rise) so the statement is not appropriate.

2 1 A This is a simple but truthful analysis of the data.
B This comment is also true but the analysis is not adequate.
2 A Although this information is true, it is not appropriate as an opening statement because it only summarizes two of the three trends.
B This statement shows the general trend over this period.

3 *Suggested answer*
With the exception of China, the percentage share of the world population rose in the developing regions between 1985 and 2005, particularly in India, whereas in Europe and North America it decreased slightly.

Language focus: Describing change over a period of time p. 40

1 A increased sharply
B fell gradually
C remained stable
D fluctuated

2 increased sharply – rose dramatically
fluctuated – varied
fell gradually – decreased steadily, fell slightly
remained stable – stayed the same

3 *shows* – present simple for general truths
rose, decreased, remained – past simple for completed actions in the past

4 1 *similar* – this means the pattern is nearly, but not exactly, the same
2 *remained relatively stable* – this is accurate
3 *lowest* – this is grammatically correct
4 *second highest* – this is a more precise way of expressing position
5 *gradually* – this is an accurate description of the trend
6 *increased slightly* – the most appropriate way of describing a little/small change

5 1 highest
2 just under
3 consistently
4 downward trend
5 decreasing steadily
6 rose progressively

6 1 *slight drop/slight fall*
  dropped/fell slightly
2 *sharp rise*
  rose sharply
3 *reached a peak*
4 *remained stable*
5 *fluctuated*
6 *sharp drop/a sharp fall*
  dropped sharply/fell sharply
7 *steady decrease/gradual fall*
  decreased steadily/fell gradually

Skills practice p. 42

Suggested answers
1 Since 2002, the percentage of people in Great Britain owning one car has remained stable at about 45 per cent of the population.
2 In 2001, about 26 per cent of the population did not have a car but in 2008 this figure had fallen to about 21 per cent.
3 From 2001 to 2007 the percentage of the population owning two or more cars increased steadily, from about 23 per cent to nearly 30 per cent.
4 Between 2007 and 2008, the percentage of British people owning two or more cars remained stable.

Selecting and grouping key information p. 43

1 A is important as it reveals the most significant information (the most popular sports for men and women). Sentences C and E are the next most relevant sentences to include as they highlight the least popular sports for both genders. Sentences B, D and F are not particularly important sentences in terms of key information.

2 Sentences B, D and E show the best ways of grouping key information as they compare and contrast the most popular sports. Although sentences A and C group information, A is too general while C is specific yet cannot really be considered as key information. Sentence F does not really group information in a logical way.

3 A This answer describes the data in a repetitive and therefore, boring style. It does not attempt to select the key information or group information clearly. This type of answer is therefore not satisfactory.

B This answer is well-organized, focuses on important information and groups key features in a logical way. Specific references to figures are provided and the language is of an appropriate academic style. It is therefore the best answer.

C Here the language is weak in terms of grammar and vocabulary: omission of articles and relative pronouns, unnecessary *to* before activity, plural forms wrong (*woman*), word formation wrong (*approximate*), inappropriate linkers used (*and* at start of sentence) and style is very repetitive (*men/women*).

Language focus: Expressing comparison and contrast p. 44

There were eight examples of the language of comparison and contrast in this sample answer.

1 swimming was the most popular sporting activity
2 whereas very few men or women enjoyed jogging
3 gym and cycling are popular with both sexes
4 for men cycling and gym are equally popular
5 and slightly more popular than football
6 while considerably more women use the gym than cycle
7 snooker is men's second favourite sport
8 it was the least popular sporting activity

Skills practice p. 44

1 1 The chart shows the percentage of UK residents who travelled from the UK to different destinations in 2007 and 2008.
2 The vertical axis represents the destination countries.
3 The horizontal axis represents the percentage of people travelling.
4 The columns show the percentage of people travelling to different destinations in 2007 and 2008.
5 The Netherlands and Cyprus are significantly more popular than any other destination.

2

From the bar charts it's easy to see most of the UK residents go on international holidays to netherlands in 2007 and 2008. Ten country had been researched and we can see that Cyprus is in second place both years.

turkey and ireland is equal popular in 2007, but Ireland visitors were not so many in 2008 and 2007. However the same number of tourist visit Turkey in this years. In 2007 Italy was the third more popular destination with 6 per cent, but is decreased to 5 per cent in 2008, the same as United states. Tourist to France is the same in 2007 and 2008. The data also shows that tourism to Netherlands is 3 or 4 times higher than others countries both in 2007 and 2008. In the two years, it has been increased slight.

Length – Approx 135 words – too short

Style – Generally OK but inappropriate use of contractions (*it's*), informal vocabulary e.g. replace *most* with *the majority*, countries not capitalized consistently.

3 Here is the corrected sample answer.

From the bar chart it is easy to see that the majority of UK tourists went to the Netherlands and Cyprus on holiday in 2007 and 2008. Ten countries were researched and we can see that Cyprus was in second place both years.

Turkey and Ireland were equally popular in 2007, but there were fewer visitors to Ireland in 2008 than in 2007. However, the same number of tourists visited Turkey in both 2007 and 2008. In 2007 Italy was the third most popular destination with 6 per cent, but this decreased to 5 per cent in 2008. The number of visitors to the United States also decreased to 5 per cent in 2008. The number of tourists visiting France was the same in 2007 and 2008.

The data also shows that in 2007 and 2008 tourism to the Netherlands was three or four times higher than in other countries. It increased slightly over the two years.

Model answer

The chart shows the percentage of UK tourists who visited a number of other countries in 2007 and 2008 on holiday. In both years the Netherlands and Cyprus were significantly more popular than the other destinations.

By far the highest percentage of tourists went to the Netherlands, with about 26 per cent visiting in 2007 and slightly more in 2008. The second most popular tourist destination was Cyprus, with a consistent 17 per cent in both years. Italy was the third most popular destination in 2007, with 6 per cent but attracted only 5 per cent of the UK tourist market in 2008. Spain and the US rose in popularity between 2007 and 2008, while tourism to Ireland fell in 2008.

France and Greece remained the least popular destinations in both years with only 2 per cent.

The chart illustrates a relatively stable pattern of tourist destinations for UK residents between 2007–2008.

(153 words)

Comments

There is a clear opening statement which has paraphrased the words describing the bar chart. The most significant features are highlighted (*By far the highest ...*) and specific details are given (*26 per cent*). Other key information is described clearly and accurately and the report finishes with an appropriate sentence to sum up the main points.

Describing a process p. 45

1 First stage: *The student contacts the institution ...*
Final stage: *The student has now enrolled ...*

2 and 3

1 The student contacts the institution about the English course. (*present simple active*)
2 The student goes to the institution and completes a placement test. (*present simple active, present simple active*)
3 The student is interviewed by an experienced teacher. (*present simple passive*)
4 The student is placed in a class at the appropriate level. (*present simple passive*)
5 The necessary forms are completed. (*present simple passive*)
6 The student's details are put on the computer. (*present simple passive*)
7 The student pays the fees for the course. (*present simple active*)
8 The student has now enrolled and is given a student card. (*present perfect active, present simple passive*)

4 A does not clearly specify what the activity is
B *improving your English* is not really a procedure – progress in English should happen after the course starts
C correct

5 *Suggested answers*
1 *Next put* a teabag into a cup.
2 *After that pour* the boiling water into the cup.
3 *After a few minutes take out* the teabag.
4 *Then add* some milk and sugar and stir.
5 *Finally drink* the tea.

6 *Sample answer*
The procedure for enrolling for an English course at a language school or college is as follows:
First of all, the student contacts the institution by phone or post about the English course. **Then** he or she goes to the school or college and completes a placement test. **After that** the person is interviewed by an experienced teacher and is placed in a class at the appropriate level, for example beginner or advanced. **At the next stage**, the necessary forms are completed **and then** the student's details are put on the computer. **Finally**, he or she is told to pay the fees for the course. **This completes the procedure** and the student has now enrolled at that particular school or college. They are given a student card and are ready to start lessons.
Note: one or two details have been added (methods of contacting the college and different levels). If you add details, they must be relevant and based on fact.

Skills practice p. 46

1   a – 10
b – 5
c – 6
d – 9
e – 2

2 *Model answer*
In order to make better quality paper from waste paper, the following process takes place:
First of all the paper is collected. After this it is very important that paper clips, plastic and staples are removed. The waste paper is then sorted into specific categories such as newspapers, computer paper and magazines. Next, the ink must be removed. This is done by soaking the paper and then breaking it up in large washers and adding chemicals. Depending on the end paper product, other materials are added such as bleach or dyes as well as other chemicals.
The materials are then passed through a heavy roller which squeezes out all the water before the pulp is pressed and flattened into thin sheets. After that these sheets are dried in furnaces and the final paper product is polished and treated before cutting into sheets or rolls. Finally the product is packaged for distribution.
(151 words)

Understanding the instructions and the question p. 47

1 A False. It is recommended, **not** compulsory.
B True. Topics are of general interest and will not be on specific subjects.
C False. Expressing views is one of the most important aspects of this task.
D True. Providing supporting evidence and information is also vital.
E False. Writing should include some personal views but aim to be academic and impersonal in style.

2 1 D
2 C

3 E
4 A
5 B

Understanding the topic and the task p. 47

1 A The question doesn't ask about visiting other countries but talks about living overseas.
B The question does not mention studying specifically.
C Correct.
2 A Correct.
B The question does not ask for a list of positive points about living overseas (although one or two could be mentioned).
C The question does not ask the candidate to compare living in the UK with other countries.

Skills practice p. 47

1 1 Main topic: high crime rates in cities
Task: suggest best ways to reduce high crime rate
2 Main topic: increased world tourism
Task: comparison of advantages and disadvantages of mass, global tourism
3 Main topic: animal testing
Task: give your opinion on whether animal testing is ever acceptable and if so, when and why

2   • to consider how things are different and how they are similar: *compare*
• to show a good reason for something: *justify*
• to compare two things to show how they are different: *contrast*
• to question whether something is true or accurate: *challenge* (*ideas*)

3 1 i – suggesting a solution to the problem of crime in cities
2 iii – comparing and contrasting the positive and negative effects of global tourism
3 ii – evaluating this view of animal testing and giving your opinions on this issue

Brainstorming and planning p. 48

1

Problems of living overseas	Ways to make living overseas easier
language	learn the language
culture and lifestyle	join a club or society
accommodation	find out about the place before you go
food and drink	sample local food
miss friends/family	keep in contact with friends/family
people	try and meet/speak to local people
religion	observe/respect local customs

2 Students' own answers
3 Students' own answers
4 C This is the most appropriate essay structure.
5 A This is the best structure because it mentions the main difficulties of living overseas in the introduction. It then describes how some problems are unavoidable in the second paragraph. It then discusses ways to make the experience easier in paragraph 3 before summing up in the final paragraph.

B This is quite well structured but the contents of paragraph 2 are not relevant to the task.

C This lacks overall structure (no conclusion) and is also irrelevant to the task.

THE INTRODUCTION p. 49

1 This opening almost repeats the question word-for-word.

2 Although giving opinions is a valid response, this introduction is too personal. The task does not require the positive points so this information is irrelevant. Exclamation marks are not appropriate in IELTS writing tasks.

3 This opening briefly mentions why people live overseas. It states that although this can be positive, certain problems are likely to occur and then gives some examples. This introduction is a balanced response to the question – the content is relevant to the task and it is written in an appropriate style.

THE MAIN BODY p. 50

1 1 Topic sentence = F
   2 Supporting evidence = A, C, D, E
   3 Link with next paragraph = B

2 *Model answer*

There is no doubt that living overseas can be very difficult at times. Adjusting to a new culture can often take weeks or months. During this period it is not uncommon for people to feel very homesick and really miss their friends and family. Not being able to speak the language very well can make life even more difficult. In addition, other problems may arise from different lifestyles, types of food or accommodation. However, there are a number of ways to reduce the difficulties.

All paragraphs should follow this basic pattern:

Topic sentence → Main idea

Supporting sentences → Supporting evidence

Concluding or bridging sentence

Sum up main idea/link to next paragraph

3 Sequencers: *firstly, secondly, finally, (thirdly, after that)* etc.
   Reason or result: *as a result, because, therefore, so, (consequently, as)* etc.
   Contrast: *however, although, despite this, (whereas)* etc.
   Extra information: *in addition, besides, moreover, (what is more, furthermore)* etc.

4 1 *Firstly* – the first suggestion
   2 *In addition* – extra information about the first suggestion (could be *secondly*)
   3 *Secondly* – the second suggestion
   4 *therefore* – a reason for the second suggestion (could be *so*)
   5 *so* – a reason for the third suggestion
   6 *However* – showing a contrast to third suggestion
   7 *Finally* – a fourth and final suggestion

5 1 find out information about the other country and speak to people who have lived abroad
   2 learn the language
   3 try to make friends with local people and keep in contact with people from your own country
   4 be open-minded

6 1 Many women have successful careers nowadays. *However*, compared to men, not many women have senior positions.

2 In England I live with a host family. *Therefore/As a result/Consequently*, my spoken English has improved rapidly.

3 Many students go overseas to study *because/as* they believe the quality of education is higher.

CONCLUSION p. 51

1 A This conclusion shows the writer's opinion in one sentence. It is clearly too brief, too general, and does not review earlier contents of the essay.

B This conclusion sums up the main idea of this task and refers back to the suggestions made earlier. The final sentence clearly illustrates the writer's view on the points discussed earlier. It is the best conclusion.

C This conclusion sums up by listing three suggestions covered in the essay and states that following these would be appropriate. The tone is too personal and listing is not really suitable in this short essay format.

2 *Model answer*

In conclusion, settling into life in a new country can cause many problems. Some difficulties cannot be avoided, for example those related to language or culture. However, there are a number of solutions such as studying the language or making friends with local people. Living abroad can often be a very positive experience and you should try to enjoy it as much as possible.

Skills practice p. 52

1 Topic: crime in cities
   Task: suggest solutions to this problem

2 *Suggested answers*

Other problems in cities	Crimes	Ways to prevent/reduce
congestion	murder	more police
overcrowding	burglary	stricter punishments
pollution	mugging	individual protection

3 Paragraph 1 – introduction – there are other problems, but crime is the biggest
   Paragraph 2 – method 1 – increase police
   Paragraph 3 – method 2 – stricter laws/punishments
   Paragraph 4 – method 3 – better security
   Paragraph 5 – conclusion – sum up ideas

4 A Too general
   B Appropriate
   C Not strictly true

5 *Model answer*

One approach would be to increase the number of police.

6 *Model answer*

This could involve increasing fines or lengthening prison sentences. If a criminal has to pay more money for doing something illegal or would face more time in prison then I believe this is likely to reduce the crime rate.

7 1 Thirdly, methods to increase security might deter potential criminals.
   2 For example, more effective alarms in houses and cars.
   3 This would reduce burglary and theft.
   4 In addition, more information about home security would also be useful.
   5 In terms of personal safety, rape alarms or even small weapons could prevent some attacks on people.

8 1 although

2 methods
3 reduced
4 would

Model answer

There is no doubt that numerous problems exist in most modern cities. Although traffic congestion, pollution and overcrowding often occur, many people believe that crime is the most serious problem in urban areas. Indeed, television and newspaper reports often tell us that crime continues to rise. However, it is possible to tackle this serious issue in a number of ways.

One approach would be to increase the number of police. If more police were on the streets, whether on foot or in patrol cars, criminals would be less likely to commit crimes and people would feel much safer. Having more police visible at night would be particularly beneficial.

A second possibility would be to make laws stricter and punishments more severe. This could involve increasing fines or lengthening prison sentences. If a criminal has to pay more money for doing something illegal or would face more time in prison then I believe this is likely to reduce the crime rate.

Thirdly, methods to increase security might deter potential criminals. For example, more effective alarms in houses and cars. This would reduce burglary and theft. In addition, more information about home security would also be useful. In terms of personal safety, rape alarms or even small weapons could prevent some attacks on people.

In conclusion, although crime is a major problem in most cities in the world, the situation can be addressed by adopting the methods mentioned above. In this way, the negative effects could be reduced and people living in cities would feel much safer.

Further practice p. 53

Model answer

Before any new product is put on the market, whether it is a cosmetic product, or a potentially life-saving medicine, the producers will want to make sure that it is safe for humans to use. A common way of doing this is to test the product on animals.

Many people feel that this is unacceptable because it assumes that an animal life is somehow less valuable than a human life. Opponents of animal testing point out that the animals involved often suffer great pain and fear, and argue that we have no right to do this to them for our own benefit.

On the other hand, it cannot be denied that animal testing has helped scientists to make great discoveries in the field of medicine, providing effective drugs against cancer, heart disease and other potentially fatal illnesses. Supporters of animal testing argue that many lives have been saved this way.

I would agree that there may be some benefits to using animals to test new medicines, although I would prefer such testing to be kept to a minimum. Increasingly, there are new ways of testing products, using cell cultures, which need not involve animals at all. However, even when this is not possible, I cannot agree that it is necessary to test cosmetic products on animals. There are already thousands of cosmetic products on the market, with no need for further development and testing. Exploiting animals in this way is, in my opinion, completely unacceptable.

In conclusion, I would not agree that testing products on animals is never acceptable, but it should be reserved for essential scientific work.

(269 words)

Comments

The essay has been clearly structured into five paragraphs: an introduction giving reasons for this situation, arguments against, arguments for, writer's opinion (strong opposition) and a clear, concise conclusion. The essay contains a wide range of grammatical structures and uses a variety of linking words to give cohesion (*on the other hand, however*). There are also numerous ways in which opinions are expressed (*Many people feel ..., I would agree ..., in my opinion ...*). Overall, the topic has been addressed thoughtfully and appropriately.

Key for Speaking module

Quiz p. 54

1 B

2 1 True
  2 False. This is not an IELTS task.
  3 True
  4 True
  5 False. You have to speak for 1–2 minutes.
  6 False. You are given a card with a topic and some prompts to help you.
  7 True
  8 True
  9 False. This is the most challenging part of the module as you are asked to talk about more abstract issues and ideas.

Talking about familiar topics p. 54

Possible questions

Your studies How long have you been studying English?

Why is it important for you to learn English?

Who was your favourite teacher at school? Why did you like their lessons?

What are you planning to study?

Why are you taking IELTS?

Your previous work experience, your current job or your future career plans

What do you do? (Be careful with this question. It means *What is your job?*)

What are/were the best things about your job?

What are your ambitions?

Your family/home life

Tell me about your family.

What does your father do? (or mother)

Do you live with your family?

Do you have a large family?

How long have you been here?

Tell me about where you are living at the moment.

Your country

How would you describe your home country/home town?

What are the best things about life in your country?

How is life in your country different from life here?

Your hobbies and interests

What are your main hobbies?

Do you enjoy travelling?

What do you usually do at the weekend?

Are you interested in playing sport?

What type of music/films do you enjoy most?

Giving a good answer p. 54

2 A Not enough information. A good example would be: *Mr Wallis, our chemistry teacher. He made the subject really interesting, and although he was very strict, he was also quite funny.*

B Doesn't answer the question. Be careful of learning phrases by heart and then just using them even when they're not appropriate. A good example would be: *I started learning English at school when I was only 10, but the lessons weren't very good. I've been studying properly for about three years though.*

C A good answer. This answers the question and adds a little extra information as well. It also sounds fluent and is accurate.

D A good answer. Again, this answers the question and gives a little extra information. The beginning, *Oh definitely ... sounds very natural.*

E Not enough information. Don't make the mistake of thinking that the less you say, the fewer mistakes you will make! The examiner needs to be able to assess your fluency and you are expected to give more than one-word answers. A good example would be: *No, I don't. I live with three other students in a shared house. It's quite close to college, so it's convenient.*

F Doesn't answer the question. Be careful with *How long* + present perfect. Remember this refers to past time up to now. A good example would be: *I came in April, so I suppose I've been here about six months now.*

G Not fluent enough. It's good to show you have a wide vocabulary, but it's more important to communicate fluently. A good example would be: *It's a small house near to the town centre. It's not very attractive, but it's comfortable and the rent's quite cheap.*

H A good answer. This answers the question, gives some extra information and is correct and fluent.

Identifying strengths and weaknesses p. 55

Although the student's answers are not monosyllabic, many of the responses are rather brief and could be more fully developed (*Five years. I studied at high school in China.*). There are a few grammatical inaccuracies (*I usually do play ping pong, the product major is charcoal*) and a rather limited range of vocabulary but some evidence of wider lexical knowledge (*managing director, fitness clubs*). Some inappropriate use of vocabulary (*charcoal town*). Pronunciation is generally good, but the intonation is heavily influenced by her native language and would benefit from flowing more freely. There aren't many words or phrases to make her responses sound more natural or to gain more time and there are quite a few hesitations. Overall, the student would need to focus on improving fluency and producing more extended responses as well as aiming to show a wider, more accurate use of language.

Planning your answer p. 56

1 and 2

Describe <u>an occasion</u> when <u>you</u> have been <u>successful</u>.
You need to talk about one occasion or event in your life (any time up to the present) when you were successful.

where and when you were successful – *give the background (school, home, college, work, how old you were)*

how you were successful – *say what happened (won a race/ passed an exam)*

what you had to do – *give examples: studied hard/worked hard/ prepared in some way/asked for help*

how you felt – *very happy because/very excited because ...*

Giving extra information p. 56

1 and 2

Talk about <u>an important day</u> in your <u>life</u>.
- <u>when</u> this day was – *about four years ago, the day my football team got promoted*
- if you were <u>alone</u> or <u>with others</u> – *with my brother and others in crowd*
- <u>where</u> you were/<u>what happened</u> – *got to football ground, waited for game to start, lots of people, final goals – we won!*
- and explain <u>why</u> this day was <u>important</u> to you – *first time team had ever been promoted*

4 *Sample answer*

OK, the important day in my life that I'm going to talk about happened **about four years ago**. This was **the day my football team got promoted**. The team, er, had played well all that season and had reached the finals, and my **brother and I** were, er, were both keen supporters and we both followed the team, er, for about 15 years. It was a very exciting day for, for the team because they'd never been promoted out of the division into a higher division in their history.

My brother and I **got into the football ground** about lunchtime and **waited for the game to start** as the crowd built up – there were about **10,000 people** there that day. The game swung from side to side, with first of all, our team scoring and then the other team scoring twice, which was why it was fantastic when **our team scored two goals in the last five minutes to win the day** and **gain promotion to the higher division**. The noise at the final whistle was amazing and we were all incredibly excited. I don't think I've ever been to a game where there was such a great atmosphere, before or since. We really celebrated that night, but the next morning, I could hardly speak from all of the shouting I'd been doing!

The speaker has included the key points and added extra details to make the talk more interesting.

5 *Sample answer*

1 Well, the **most important present I ever got** was **a smartphone** with a touch screen and all sorts of apps! I think it's amazing to be able to go online, text, phone and chat with my friends on my favourite social network. I can make video calls to friends abroad and talk to my family for free. **My husband** gave it to me **for my birthday**. He knew I wanted one, because I was always looking at them in the shops and saying how useful it would be to be able to read my emails wherever I was. So, when it was coming up to my birthday he took me to the mobile phone shop and asked me to look at the different types of smartphone. But I already knew which one I wanted. So it didn't take any time at all to choose. I was so excited with it when I first got it! I just couldn't stop checking it and adding new songs to the playlists. **The thing I really like about it is that I can be in touch with my friends and my family all the time and keep up with work whenever I like** without having to be near a computer. And what's fantastic ... I can read books on my phone as well. And, one more thing that I didn't expect ... I'm actually listening to more music than I used to. So, my phone's really very important to me.

This answer is the right length and includes all the points in the instruction.

2

Student 1

I met my friend in China six years ago. My parents and his parents are, um, workmates and he and me are, were, classmates in high school. And, um, he's in England for three years, and so am I. Er, we study together and live together as well. He studies harder than me and he's, er, very generous and he's, er, quite intelligent as well. So he plays a very important place in my life.

Student 2

OK. I have a friend called Jolie. She's Chinese and we met in the first class, the first English class. We were paired up to do an assignment and that's how we became friends. Umm … I've known her for about five months and it's been fun. We do … we help each other with assignments and we go for movies and cook together, have dinners and stuff and just have fun talking, laughing and singing. Um … I think she's played a very important part in my life because she … she … I admire her motivation and dedication and I think she's a very intelligent person and very strong-willed and … something … a lot of her character I wish I had in my life so that's why I think she's played an important role in my life.

Identifying strengths and weaknesses p. 57

Student 1

This answer is quite short and does not satisfactorily cover all the points on the card. However, it has quite a good range of language and is quite accurate.

Student 2

Level of communicative ability is high. Some hesitations but clear that the speaker has a very natural style and produces a measured, thoughtful response to the points on the card.

Follow-up questions p. 57

1   1D 2E 3C 4F 5B 6A

Expanding answers p. 57

Model answers

1 **Is it a good idea to exercise regularly?** Yes, I think it's a good idea – especially as you get older because it can help to keep your body active. It's important to make time for exercise, even when you're busy, so I try to go to the gym three times a week. If I'm honest, however, it's usually more like twice a week.

2 **Is there more crime these days?** Well, no, I don't think there is really. It probably just seems that way because it's reported in all the newspapers and on the television. I think there has always been quite a lot of crime in big cities, although there may be more crime such as house-breaking in rural communities these days.

3 **Do you think children should have mobile phones?** Well, I think it can be useful for children to have a mobile to keep in touch with their parents. On the other hand, mobiles can be very distracting and a lot of children just use them as toys. But if parents and teachers can control how and when children use them, I think they're quite a good idea.

Linking ideas p. 58

1 1 because
2 so
3 and
4 however, on the other hand
5 such as

3 *Sample answers and commentary*

1 Do you think it's important for young people to spend time with older people?
Yes. I think young people can learn a lot from older people. For instance, older people have plenty of experience and can give advice on all sorts of problems. On the other hand, younger people have loads of energy and curiosity that they can share with the older generation.
This is a full answer. The student uses a range of relevant vocabulary (*experience, advice, problems, energy, curiosity, generation*) and linking phrases (*for instance, on the other hand*). The grammar is correct.

2 Do you think children should learn financial planning at school or at home?
My family save its money, but many people is spending all the time. The teachers should teach the students to save.
This is very short, but the student has tried to answer the question (*family, save, spending, teachers, students*). There is no extension and there is only one linking word (*but*). The grammar is inaccurate (*family save, people is spending*).

3 Can you think of some of the negative effects of text messaging?
Well, I think text messages are quite, how do you say … not friendly. Because, you send a funny message, and the other person don't know how you feel and they don't think you joking and get upset with you.
This answer is quite good, but needs more extension. The student has only given one example of a misunderstanding and has only included one link (*because*). There isn't a wide range of vocabulary (*not friendly* = impersonal). There are a few grammar mistakes (*person don't know, you joking, get upset*).

4 Which is better: living in the countryside or in the city?
Personally, I like living in the countryside. I like the peace and quiet. But then, on the other hand, you don't have the same facilities in the countryside, like transport and shops. So I suppose that it's actually more practical to live in the city.
This answer is a good introduction. It could be extended with more discussion of the benefits of living in the city. There are several linking words (*but then, on the other hand, so*) and expressions that make the speaker sound quite fluent (*personally, but then, I suppose, actually*). The grammar is correct.

5 To what extent are qualifications important?
Qualifications are important to get a job. For example, I'm a doctor. I couldn't get a job without qualifications.
This is very short and only answers part of the question. It should be extended to include other advantages and limitations of qualifications. The vocabulary is limited (*qualifications* repeated from the question and *job* and *doctor*). The grammar is correct, but very simple. There is only one linking phrase (*for example*).

6 How likely is it that computers will be able to replace humans in the workplace?
Computers have already replaced humans in a lot of ways. For example, in car manufacturing, robots do a lot of the finishing and assembly, where, in the past people did the

work. But I don't think computers can take the place of people completely because there are certain jobs, such as nursing, that really need human contact.

This is a full answer. It includes a range of relevant vocabulary (*manufacturing, robots, finishing, assembling, nursing, human contact*) and linking words (*for example, where, in the past, but, because, such as*). The grammar is correct.

7 Would you prefer to watch sport or play it?
Actually, I'm not like sport. I not watching it or play it. I play computer game online. My favourite is X Men. I play with my friends every night.

This is too short and does not answer the question. The vocabulary is limited and repetitive (*play*). The sentence forms are very simple and there are no linking words. There are several grammar errors (*I'm not like, I not watching/play, computer game*).

8 How do you think global warming will affect transport in the future?
One possibility is that it can become more and more expensive to travel and people cannot to go to other countries so often. Another possibility is that we can have new kinds of transport with wind, solar and hydrogen power.

This is a good start but the answer could be extended with more discussion. There is only one link between the ideas (*another possibility*). There is a range of relevant vocabulary (*travel, other countries, wind, solar and hydrogen power*). There are some grammar errors (*it can become* = it may/will become, *people cannot to go* = may/will not be able to go, *can have* = may/will have).

Key for Practice test

Listening

1 C
2 B
3 £72
4 no
5 [security] deposit
6 [number of] drivers
7 C
8 Drysdale (NOT Drisdale)
9 8.00 a.m.
10 357629
11 7.00/7.00 to 9.00
12 fitness suite
13 weight lifting/weight-lifting
14 headphone connections
15 trained instructors/instructors
16 C
17 C
18 B
19 limited access
20 credit card
21 Law
22 globalization of crime
23 international crime
24 richest countries
25 victim
26 agent
27 client

28 poaching and killing
29 regional level
30 policies and regulations
31 space exploration
32 medicine
33 water purification systems
34 space craft
35 fire resistant
36 weather conditions
37 air traffic control
38 exploring
39 Global warming
40 C

Reading

1 experimental
2 transmission
3 weather
4 sound
5 entertainment
6 Yes
7 Yes
8 Not given
9 No
10 No
11 C
12 D
13 A
14 first published
15 second edition
16 available online
17 store words electronically
18 outlets
19 300,000
20 D
21 B
22 C
23 vi
24 viii
25 iii
26 D
27 F
28 C
29 E
30 D
31 F
32 C
33 No It is designed with psychologists from the universities of Oxford and Cambridge.
34 Not given
35 Yes
36 Yes
37 mindfulness
38 concentration
39 calmer
40 anxiety

Writing

Model answer for Task 1

The chart indicates how people in different age groups spent their free time during 2007–2008. In general, the most popular leisure activity was watching television, while the least popular, overall, was reading.

However, there were exceptions to these trends, specifically in the 16–24 and 65+ age groups. In the youngest group, listening to music (about 83 per cent) was marginally more popular than watching television (about 82 per cent), while in the oldest group reading (73 per cent) was second to watching television (90 per cent).

It can be seen that reading was the least popular activity with 16–24 year olds (only 46 per cent), but became more popular with age. Listening to music, on the other hand, became gradually less popular as people aged and was the least common pastime in the 65+ age group (62 per cent). At just over 60 per cent, shopping was almost equally popular with all groups.

In summary, as people aged, watching television and reading became more popular while listening to music became less so.

(163 words)

Model answer for Task 2

It is widely accepted that global warming has been caused by releasing CO_2 into the atmosphere. Therefore, over the last century it has become increasingly important to consider the environmental effects of manufacturing consumer goods. However, the responsibility not only lies with the manufacturer, but also with the consumer. I agree that we should take environmental factors into account when we shop, but I think that our decisions are limited by practical considerations.

When we buy certain products we should be aware of their carbon footprint, the amount of carbon that is emitted when they are produced or transported. For example, vegetables that are transported from the other side of the world or farming methods that use large quantities of chemicals. Additionally, we should take packaging into account, as it is usually made of some form of plastic, which often cannot be recycled.

On the other hand, although it is important to consider all the factors mentioned above, it is not always possible to avoid products with a high carbon footprint, for practical reasons such as cost, variety and information. Goods with a low carbon footprint are often more expensive, as they have higher production costs, and if we want to avoid fruit and vegetables from countries far away, our choice will be limited by the climate in our region. Furthermore, we have relatively little information about the carbon footprint of most products.

In conclusion, although it would be ideal to purchase products with a low carbon footprint, there are practical limitations, and we often have to reach a compromise between the two.

(262 words)

Listening module

Recording 01

[K = Keiko, S = Stephan]

K: Um, excuse me. Do you know where the accommodation office is?

S: Yes, of course. Are you a new student?

K: Yeah. I only arrived here yesterday, so I still feel a bit lost.

S: I've only been here a couple of weeks, but it doesn't take long to find your way around. The campus isn't that big. The accommodation office is in the main building.

K: Is that the three-storey building by the lake?

S: No – look, it's that big building, there behind the trees. The one with the glass front. Go in through the main door – then up the steps.

K: You mean the door on the right-hand side?

S: Yeah. Then, when you get inside, go straight down the corridor, to the far end, and turn left. You'll see three doors on your left – accommodation is the middle one.

K: So, I go along the corridor, turn left, and it's the second door on the left?

S: That's right!

K: Thanks very much for your help.

S: No problem, see you around. My name is Stephan, by the way.

K: Oh, OK, great. I'm Keiko.

Recording 02

[K = Keiko, AO = Accommodation Officer]

K: Excuse me, am I in the right place to look for accommodation?

AO: Are you a student here?

K: Yes, I just arrived yesterday, and I was looking for some help with finding a place to live.

AO: Well, you've come to the right place! What sort of accommodation are you looking for?

K: I'm not sure really. Could you tell me what's available?

AO: Of course. There are three kinds of accommodation that we deal with – home stays, college halls of residence, or private lets.

K: Home stays? Is that where you live with a family?

AO: Yes, that's right. Usually you have your own room, and maybe your own bathroom, but you live with a local family and they provide you with meals, access to a washing machine, all of that kind of thing. That's £130 per week, or £90 without meals.

K: Yes, I did think about doing that. It would be a good way to practise my English, but I think I'd really prefer to live with people more my own age, other students, for example.

AO: Of course. Well, the college has a small residential block, with rooms for 50 students, but it's very popular and I think at the moment it's full.

K: That's a shame.

AO: Yeah, students like it. You have your own study bedroom, with a bed, a table, chair and a washbasin, and then you share a bathroom and kitchen with four other students.

K: It sounds nice. Never mind. What was the other option that you mentioned?

AO: The other one is, um, private lets. These are flats and houses owned by private landlords, not the college, but we make sure that you are paying a reasonable price so it's a bit easier than just looking in the newspaper to find a flat.

K: That sounds good. Would it be for one person or more?

AO: It depends. Mostly, flats are for three to four students, but there are sometimes one-bedroom flats available.

Recording 03

[K = Keiko, AO = Accommodation Officer]

K: So, how can I find out about the flats or rooms that are available at the moment?

AO: Well, I can give you all that, but if you wouldn't mind, first of all, I'll take down a few contact details and then if something suitable comes up, I'll be able to tell you.

K: OK, great.

AO: So, what's your name, please?

K: Keiko Jenkins.

AO: Sorry, could you spell that for me, please?

K: Of course. It's K-E-I-K-O and my surname is J-E-N-K-I-N-S.

AO: Thank you. What's your nationality? I thought that you must be Japanese, but Jenkins is an English name.

K: Yes, it is. My father is English, and I have British nationality, but I grew up in Japan, so I feel more Japanese.

AO: How interesting. So, Keiko, where are you staying at the moment?

K: At the Sunrise Guest House. It's number 562 Green Park Road.

AO: 562 Green Park Road. Fine. And do you have a contact number?

K: I've got a mobile. It's 07785 265 981.

AO: Sorry, I didn't quite get that. Was it 256 891?

K: No, 07785 265 981.

AO: Thanks. And email? Have you got an address you can access easily?

K: Yeah, it's keiko@hotmail.com

AO: That's fine. OK …

Recording 04

15
50
162
£3.25
47%
0.54
12,651

Recording 05

U Y J O G X I P Z W H A Q R E B

Recording 06

1 forward slash
2 hyphen
3 colon
4 semi-colon
5 dot

Recording 07

1 A: Sorry. What was that name again – Sir Anthony … ?
  B: Sir Anthony Winton, that's A-N-T-H-O-N-Y. W-I-N-T-O-N.
2 A: So what's the answer, then?
  B: 34.92.
3 A: Could I just take your address?
  B: Certainly, it's 15 Sparrow Lane. Sparrow is S-P-A-double R-O-W.
4 A: How high is Everest?
  B: Let me look it up. Mm, it says here 29,030 feet.
5 A: What's his name again?
  B: Michael MacWilliams – M-I-C-H-A-E-L M-A-C-W-I-double L-I-A-M-S.
6 A: … and I live at 286 Banbury Road.
  B: How do you spell Banbury?
  A: B-A-N-B-U-R-Y.
  B: Thanks.
7 A: So, what did I get in the test?
  B: 74%.
  A: Great!
8 A: Who's your favourite author?
  B: Mm, that's hard, but I think it must be Janet Gates.
9 A: So, what was the number again?
  B: 0121 674 9544.
10 A: Do you have a reference number on that letter?
  B: Um, yes, I think so. Here it is … reference number 654/120084.
11 A: OK, is it Mrs J Smith?
  B: No. Mrs J Robson-Smith.
12 A: … and what's your address there?
  B: Flat 3, 547 Oxford Road.
13 A: What was the web address of that company?
  B: I think it was www.bht.co.uk
14 A: Could I make an appointment, please?
  B: Which doctor do you usually see?
  A: Dr Brown.
15 A: What's the registration of the car?
  B: N770 CES.

Recording 08

[RM = Restaurant Manager, D = Dan]
RM: Hello, Giovanni's Italian Restaurant. Can I help you?
D: Hello, yes, I hope so. I'm phoning to enquire about booking a party at your restaurant. Do you cater for large groups?
RM: Yes, we do, but the maximum we can seat together is 24.
D: Oh, that's fine. I think there'll be about 18 of us.
RM: Fine, no problem. We have a large room at the back of the restaurant that we usually use for groups. It means that you are not disturbed by the other customers.
D: That sounds fantastic. Does it cost extra for that?
RM: No, no, no, we just ask that you spend at least £10 per person on your meal.
D: That seems reasonable. Is it one long table?

RM: No, it's three round tables. Each table will seat eight people. We find that's a bit more of a friendly way of eating – you can talk to more people, and there's more space on the table for the food!
D: Oh, yes – that's important!
RM: So, when do you want to come?
D: Well, we'd like a Friday or Saturday night really, maybe April the 15th?
RM: Let me see. Oh, I'm sorry, the 15th is already fully booked. I have a space on the 16th – that's the Saturday. Is that any good?
D: It's not really what we wanted, but it'll be OK.
RM: Or the week before? I have a space on Friday the 8th.
D: That's a bit early, really. No, the 16th will be fine.
RM: Usually when we have larger groups we do a set menu – three courses and coffee for a fixed price. Is that what you were looking for?
D: Is there any choice about the different courses?
RM: But of course! We don't expect everyone to want exactly the same thing! For each course there is a choice of three different dishes, it may be a prawn cocktail to start with for example, or a soup, or maybe a plate of Italian ham and cold meat – we call it *antipasto*.
D: Great. Just one other thing … I know that a few people in the group are vegetarian. Do you do a vegetarian option?
RM: Absolutely. At least one of the choices for each course is made without meat or fish.
D: That all sounds great. Is coffee included in the price, did you say?
RM: Certainly … cappuccino, espresso, whatever you like.
D: OK. So how much do you usually charge for the set menu?
RM: For parties of under ten people, it's £15 a head. If you have more than ten, it's a bit cheaper!
D: As I said, I think it'll be about 18 people.
RM: In that case, we can do it for £12 a head. That doesn't include wine or drinks, of course.
D: No, I understand. Well, that all sounds very good.
RM: There's only one other thing – for larger groups like this, we like to take a deposit a week before you are planning to come – 10% would be fine.
D: Oh, OK. 10% – that'd be 10% of £12 multiplied by 18 people … how much is that?
RM: Wait, I have a calculator here … um … it's £21.60. Call it £25 to make it a round number.
D: OK, so I need to give you £25 a week before the 16th of April?
RM: Perfect!
D: Right, well, I'll finalize the numbers and get back to you in the next couple of weeks to give you the deposit.
RM: Lovely. We look forward to your visit, Mr …
D: Glover, Dan Glover.
RM: Sorry, can you spell that, Mr Glover?
D: Sure, it's G-L-O-V-E-R.
RM: Thank you. And could I take a contact telephone number for you?
D: Of course. My work number is probably best – it's 01452 863092.
RM: Thank you very much. We look forward to seeing you.
D: Goodbye.

Recording 09

Hello again, and welcome to *You can do it*, the programme that aims to help give you inside information into life's trickier tasks. Today we're going to talk about the different ways there are of buying a used car, something that very few people feel very confident about. And let's face it, a mistake can be expensive, as well as very inconvenient.

So your old car has broken down again, and you're feeling that this really is the end for it and it's not worth repairing, or maybe you've just passed your test and are desperate to get out on the road. You look at new cars, but they are so expensive – what can you do? Well, there are three main places to look for a used car, and they all have their advantages and their disadvantages. The first place, and probably the one that most people would go to first, is a used car dealer. These are showrooms where you can go and choose from a range of second-hand cars. Obviously some places are bigger than others, and some are better than others. On the whole, this kind of place is probably the safest way of buying a car as you'll get some kind of warranty. Typically this is about three to six months, maybe a year on a newer car, so if something goes wrong with the car after you've bought it you can take it back – you've got some kind of guarantee. The problem, of course, is that you'll pay for it. Cars from dealers are usually about 800 to £1,000 more expensive than the same type of car bought privately. Quite often, dealers will offer you a discount, especially if you've got an old car to trade in, and that might make it seem very attractive. Many will offer you credit, too, so that you don't have to pay for the car straightaway, but it's always good to remember that although this is an expensive way to buy a car, it's probably the safest.

Recording 10

If you're looking for a cheaper car, one way to go about it is to buy a car privately – usually by looking in the adverts in your local paper. This can be a really good way of buying a car, but takes quite a bit more effort. You have to get the paper each week, look through all of the adverts to see if there is anything suitable, make phone calls to arrange a time to see the car, and then travel to view it. The obvious problem is that once you've bought the car it's yours and you can't really take it back. It's probably a really good idea, if you know nothing about cars, to get a mechanic to check it over for you before you buy it.

The final place that you can buy cars is at auction. There are auction rooms up and down the country where cars are sold to whoever will pay the highest price for them. This is definitely the cheapest way of buying a car, but it's also the most risky because you won't really have time to check the car over. So unless you're a mechanic, or don't mind taking a risk, this probably isn't the best way of buying a car. You can find some real bargains, though!

Well, we're now going over to our reporters who have been trying out these different methods. Let's hear what they think …

Recording 11

Good morning, everyone. It's good of you all to come, especially those of you who have come straight from sports coaching. For those of you who don't know me, my name is Jenny Arnold and I'm the university Health and Fitness Officer. Today we've got another in our series of occasional health lectures. This time, with the summer drawing closer and many of you off on holiday, I wanted to talk a bit about being safe and keeping healthy while you're travelling.

Actually, the time to start thinking about this is a few weeks before you go away. If you're going to a foreign country, it's a really good idea to check out any vaccinations that you need. Your GP can tell you about this, or you can call up NHS Direct, the free medical telephone service and talk to one of the nurses there. Don't leave it until the last minute, because for some of the vaccinations you'll have to have two shots with a week or two between them. Your local doctor, as well as giving you advice, can give you most of these injections and they should be free as you're students, but you may have to pay for things like malaria tablets if you are going to a country where malaria is a problem.

The other thing that you should arrange before you leave is travel insurance. You might think that this is a waste of money, and it can be quite expensive if you are going somewhere exotic, or doing dangerous sports or activities such as diving or skiing. But it does mean that you can relax and enjoy your holiday, knowing that if anything terrible did happen to you, then you'd be covered financially, at least, and could get home safely.

While you are away, especially if you are going somewhere hot, as many of you probably want to, then do take care in the sun. Most of us here in the UK, don't see much sunshine for most of the year, and if you suddenly expose your skin to the midday sun, without any sun cream, you'll just end up looking very red and feeling very sore. It's not a good start to your holiday and there can be dangerous long-term consequences from skin cancer, too.

Finally, take a few sensible precautions about eating and drinking to avoid illness. Be careful about drinking the water if you are visiting less developed countries and remember that this includes things like cleaning your teeth and ice in your drinks. It's always fun to try new food when you're away, but you might find that you have a slightly upset stomach for the first couple of days, just while you get used to it. Make sure that you keep drinking plenty of liquid – bottled water is best, but soft drinks and fruit juice are OK in moderation too. Take a couple of tablets for it if it gets very bad. You can get these from any chemist here.

Well, I hope that that's been helpful. If you have any other questions, I'm in room 5B. Just pop in and ask me.

Recording 12

[R = Robert, A = Anand, C = Claire]
R: Hi there, Anand. What are you up to?
A: Hi, Robert. Hi, Claire. I'm just having a look at the group project that we've got to do this term.
C: The ecology one?
A: Mm, that's the one.
R: Well, we've probably caught you at a good time then. Claire and I were hoping we could have a bit of a chat about it with you. We're doing it together, aren't we? Have you got a minute now, or are you busy?
A: No, it's OK. Now is a good time. We do need to think about starting work on it, don't we?
C: The main question seems to be knowing where to start. I know that we have to identify an environmental problem somewhere in the world, and look at what kind of measures have been taken to limit it, but it's difficult to narrow it down to one!

Recording 13

[R = Robert, A = Anand, C = Claire]

A: Yeah, trying to think of a topic is a problem, isn't it? I've been thinking about it, but it was only the major disasters that I could think of – you know the recent ones that have been in the news.

R: Like what?

A: Oh, you know, water pollution like the oil tanker that broke up and killed all the sea life for miles near Spain, or the kind of thing that's always talked about, like global warming.

C: Do you think we should choose something like that?

A: No! It'd be such a major piece of work if we did.

R: What's the word limit again? Is it 1,500 words, as usual?

A: No, this one's 500 words longer.

C: 2,000? Help! We've got more work than I thought!

A: Have you got any ideas for a topic?

R: One or two. I was having trouble, too, I looked through books in the library and some journals, but what worked in the end was an internet search.

A: What did you search for?

R: I put in *environmental* and *disaster* and then did some other searches using words like *sea*, or *river* or *soil erosion*.

A: And that helped?

R: Well, sort of! It gave me a lot of information. My first search came up with 372,000 sites! Obviously I didn't look through them all, but browsing through some gave me an idea for the assignment. How about looking at the problems of pollution in Sydney Harbour?

Recording 14

[R = Robert, A = Anand, C = Claire]

C: The harbour? It'd be local, but it looks pretty clean to me!

R: It is now, but it used to be a real problem. Sewage, for example, used to be emptied directly into the harbour.

A: Yuck! Imagine swimming in all of that waste water. It's not a nice thought, is it?

C: You said it used to be a problem …

R: Yes. Sewage is taken out in pipes a long way out to sea now. The City Council constructed them in the 1970s. Unless there is very bad weather, it's solved the problem.

C: What other problems are there?

R: Well, of course there is a fair bit of pollution from the traffic in the harbour.

C: You mean all of the boats?

R: Yes. There are the ferries, of course, but also the commercial and trading vessels. It's still an issue. The state government has set targets for reduction in emissions by next year, but they can't stop boats using the harbour, can they?

A: I guess one of the other problems must just be people dumping rubbish – bottles, plastic bags, stuff that people can't be bothered to dispose of properly.

R: Yeah, that's right. There's quite a good story behind that one, though. It's an ongoing project – it's not finished yet, but a lot of it has been removed.

C: How did they manage that? It must be a really difficult job.

R: Local diving clubs who like to dive in the Harbour go down and pick up old bottles and things like that off the bottom of the sea. I think they have a special day once a year to do it.

Recording 15

[R = Robert, A = Anand, C = Claire]

A: So, do you think those are the three main areas we should look at for our assignment?

R: Well, that seems to make sense to me, at least it's reasonably limited.

C: I think we should make some notes, so that we can divide up the work.

A: Yeah, that's a good idea. So, tell us again, what do the divers do?

R: It's in their interests, really – they want to dive in clean water, so they go down and pick up old bottles and cans, things like that. I think that they leave the rubbish if any marine life has started living in it – they wouldn't want to make a crab homeless!

C: That's great, isn't it?

A: So the Harbour is really clean, now?

R: Well, not bad. When the weather is bad, especially if there's a lot of rain and a wind blowing towards the shore, the sewage can still be blown in to the beaches.

C: Not very nice … but I suppose it's not very often. I heard that people using jet skis and small motor boats was a problem.

R: Yeah, I read about that, too. Emissions are actually getting worse, despite what the government wants to happen.

C: You would think that that kind of thing would make people who live here really angry.

R: You would, but actually, they get much more bothered when they have to swim in waste water, after a storm …

Recording 16

1 The college is on the site of an old castle.
2 The meeting will be held on the sixth of February.
3 Please hand your essays in by next Wednesday.
4 We suggest that you take the test in May.
5 The course is inexpensive and highly beneficial.
6 Unemployment rose dramatically in 2001.
7 I would advise you to do your homework.
8 He was a very successful politician.
9 Different companies have different management systems.
10 The maths exam was easier than the statistics test.
11 Studying abroad can help you become more independent.
12 Receiving unwanted emails, or *spam*, is a growing problem.

Recording 17

[B = Brenda, C = Cathy]

B: Hi, Cathy, I haven't seen you around for ages. Where have you been?

C: Oh, I've been here, but I've been studying really hard, and not going out much, so that's probably why I haven't seen you. I seem to spend all of my time in the library, or in my room with my nose in a book!

B: So your course is hard work?

C: Yes, it is, but it's mainly because we're coming to the end of the year and I've got a few major assignments to get in.

B: Actually, I wanted to talk to you about your course. You're on the Foundation Programme, aren't you?

C: Yeah, that's right. Are you thinking of doing it next year?

B: Maybe. I want to study at a British university, but I'm not sure whether it would be better to do 'A' levels, or a Foundation Course. Which do you think would be better?

C: Well, the big advantage of a Foundation Course is that it only takes a year – 'A' levels take two.

B: Really? That's a big difference!

C: Mm, it is. With 'A' levels, you usually study two or three subjects, and you may not get any extra language support. With a Foundation, you study five or six modules, but they are all connected to one subject – usually the one you want to study at university, for example Business, or IT, and you do extra English classes, too – mostly about six hours a week.

B: That sounds helpful.

C: And another good thing about it is that you don't have to take any exams on the Foundation Course – well, not any major ones, anyway. All the marks come from continuous assessment, you know, from your assignments and presentations, that kind of thing. 'A' levels have some continuous assessment, but a lot of your marks come from the final exam.

B: That's a bit scary ... So, if the Foundation Course is so much shorter and has no exams, why would anyone want to do 'A' levels?

C: Good question. I didn't want to and Foundation Courses tend to be popular with students from overseas, but I think most British students do 'A' levels. It's part of their education system. Also, to be honest, if you get good 'A' levels, it gives you a lot more choice about which university you can go to. All British universities recognize 'A' levels, but some don't recognize Foundation Courses, especially if you want to do one of the more popular courses.

B: So you are saying it's hard to find a place at a university with a Foundation Course?

C: No, there is still a lot of choice, just not as much as with 'A' levels.

B: What's the course like anyway?

C: Hard work! But I've enjoyed it. The one I'm doing combines Business Studies and English, so I study different business modules for 15 hours a week, and then we study Academic English – that's six hours.

B: And what are the English classes like?

C: They're good – I find them really helpful. They're not like the general English classes I was doing before, though. We do a lot of work on reading academic-type texts and writing in the sort of style that you need to use at university. It's quite hard. Even when I feel that the language I'm using is mainly accurate, the thing that's really different to my language is how essays are structured in English. We're doing quite a bit of IELTS practice, too, at the moment, because most of us are planning to take it next month.

B: So you have to take the IELTS exam?

C: Most universities want you to, yes.

B: What's the other part of the course like?

C: The business modules? They're really interesting. We look at economic theory and marketing strategies, global markets, all kinds of things. I had a bit of an advantage, because I studied Business in high school in France and so I know some of the information already, but it's in a bit more depth than I did before and studying it in English makes a big difference. It can be difficult to understand everything that your lecturer says sometimes. We have a lot of written work to give in too – assignments, mainly.

B: It sounds very hard.

C: And I've got to give a 20 minute presentation next week using PowerPoint ...

B: Really?

C: But despite all of that I'm really enjoying it!

B: So have you applied for any universities, yet?

C: Yes, but it's difficult, because the university I really want to go to hasn't given me an offer yet.

B: Which one is that?

C: Ainsley University. I've had a conditional offer from Millford, and they only want IELTS band 5.5, which I'm sure I can get. I've heard that Ainsley usually ask for 6.5, and that's a bit more difficult. Then there's Parmouth, but I haven't heard from them yet, either.

B: Which one is the better university?

C: Overall, Ainsley is, but people say that Millford has a great Business School.

B: What's Millford like as a place to live?

C: Well, it's in Westhampton, actually. I've heard the city is pretty good, but Parmouth is better – it's close to the sea.

Recording 18

Diagram 1

So, light rays from the object, which is a small leaf in this illustration, come through the lens to the eye, but because they are diffracted, or bent by the lens, the eye sees a virtual image, which is closer and smaller than the real object.

Diagram 2

Pendulum clocks have always been popular. Their technology is quite straightforward, as we can see if we look at this diagram. You can see the hour and minute hands on the front of the clock, we call this the *clock face*, and then if we look behind the face, we see the main gear train, and behind that, the *pendulum*. That's P-E-N-D-U-L-U-M. This is the part of the clock that we hear ticking. This is driven by a weight, which is situated in front of the pendulum and by slowly pulling downwards on a string, the weight pulls the gear train around.

Diagram 3

The campus is quite a large one, and most people take a few days to find their way around. The Students' Union is the large, single storey building in the middle of the campus, and the cafeteria is right behind it. You can get to the cafeteria through the Students' Union, or through a separate entrance at the back. If you walk out of the main entrance to the Union, there is a large lawn area that is very popular in the summer, and then, to your left is the library, and over to your right is the Porter Building.

Recording 19

Good morning, everyone. Well, moving on from our discussion last week about oil-fired power stations, I want to move on today to a form of power that many would argue is far superior. It provides 25% of all electricity worldwide and is the only power generator in common use that uses renewable energy – I am, of course, talking about hydroelectric or hydropower plants – energy from water. Hydropower plants are actually based on a rather simple concept – water flowing through a dam turns a turbine, which turns a generator. The idea is nothing more than a water wheel and the principle has been in use for thousands of years.

Some hydropower plants are built using waterfalls, but the majority of them rely on a dam that holds back the water in a river, and creates a large artificial lake, called a reservoir. That's R-E-S-E-R-V-O-I-R. If you look at this diagram, you will see that the main power house is built in front of the dam and that the transformer is inside, seated on the generator. The turbine is situated underground. Sorry, what was that? Oh, turbine, T-U-R-B-I-N-E. Right, as you can see, under the dam there is a control gate, and this can be opened to let the water in. It travels by gravity, through a tunnel, called the *penstock*, to the turbine, and then out of the outflow to the river below the dam. This movement of water turns the turbine, which generates electricity. The amount of power generated can be controlled by the amount of water taken in by the control gate, so that, for example, at night, when less electricity is consumed, the supply can also be reduced. The power is converted by the transformer into very high voltage current, which is then taken to where it's needed by the power lines, shown leading away from the power station.

Recording 20

Let's look at this final process in a little more detail. As we've said, the power leaves the generator and enters what is known as a *transmission substation* at the power plant. This substation uses large transformers to convert the electricity up to extremely high voltages. This may be over a hundred thousand volts. The reason for this is to reduce losses of power when it's transported over very long distances. On average, electricity travels about 500 km from where it's produced to where it's used. That's a long way! The next stage in the process is a local power substation. This has several functions – it 'steps down' the electric voltage, that is, it reduces it to something that can be used domestically, it also distributes the power, and finally, has circuit breakers so that the power can be switched off if necessary. The power coming out of the substation and along wires to houses is still at 7,200 volts, and so, close to each house, is a transformer drum or box, which lowers the voltage to 240 volts – normal domestic electric service. Finally, each house has a fuse box, or a circuit breaker, which are safety devices to ensure that accidents with electricity are minimized in the home.

Recording 21

Let's get back to our hydroelectric plant. One of the main advantages, of course, of generating power in this way, is that it is a very clean and green method. It takes advantage of a naturally occurring process and so there is little pollution caused, and it's sustainable – it will keep going long after coal and oil have run out. However, there are some difficulties. It depends a lot on the geography of the country – obviously a large river is needed with a reliable flow of water and it's often difficult to find a place which is suitable for a dam. Creating a large, artificial lake involves flooding a river valley, and this is not often popular with the people whose homes will be left underwater! Usually people are compensated and resettled – given homes in a new location – but this can cause other social problems.

Recording 22

Good afternoon. Today we start the first in a series of five lectures on the petroleum industry. Today we'll be looking at how oil is formed, and how it's found by oil companies. Over the next few weeks we'll be examining the process of extraction, and of processing, in more depth.

Right, as you know, in the developed world in particular, oil is a vital commodity. In a single month, the demand for crude oil in the USA can be over 400 million barrels. So where does it come from? And how did it get there? Between 10 million and 600 million years ago oil was formed from the remains of tiny plants and animals, mostly invisible to the human eye, called *plankton*. When they died, the plankton sank to the bottom of the sea, into the sand and mud. Because of all the sand and mud, usually called *sediment*, there was little or no oxygen and so the plankton was broken down to form organic layers. We call this mixture of organic matter and rock, *source rock*. Over millions of years, more and more sediment was deposited, and the weight of these layers put enormous pressure and heat on the source rock. Because of this, the organic matter, which, you will remember was originally from our plankton, was distilled into crude oil, and could flow out of the rock. Some rock, such as sandstone, is very porous, which means that liquid can be absorbed into it, a bit like a sponge. The crude oil collects in rock like sandstone, or perhaps limestone, and it is called *reservoir rock*.

So what we have now is crude oil, inside sandstone, or maybe limestone, under the ground. Now, if you look at the diagram on your handouts, you'll see that this reservoir rock can be trapped in the Earth by various methods. In all three cases, the natural gas and oil is trapped below a layer of hard rock that it can't flow through. This is known as *cap rock*. The first illustration shows *folding*; strong horizontal movements push the rock together into a fold and trap the oil and the natural gas, which sits on top of it. The second drawing shows *faulting*, that's F-A-U-L-T-I-N-G. Here the layers of rock crack, and then, when one side shifts upwards or downwards, the oil is trapped against the fault line. Thirdly, we have *pinching out*. In this case the cap rock comes up from below, and is actually squeezed upwards into the reservoir rock, leaving two pockets of oil.

Finding oil is an expensive business, and although modern technology, such as satellite imaging, has made it much easier, the success rate for finding oil fields is still remarkably low. For every ten potential sites found, only one will yield a new oil field. When one has been found, however, there are certain procedures that need to be followed. The first thing is to settle all the legal issues over who owns the land. As drilling is usually in desert areas or the sea, this is not always as straightforward as you might think! After this has been done, the crew start to prepare to drill. Let's look at a land example to give us the idea. Firstly, the land has to be cleared and levelled and access roads may have to be built, depending on what is available. Water is needed for the drilling process, so there must be a source of it locally. If there isn't one, then a well has to be dug. After this, the crew dig a *reserve pit* – basically a big hole lined with plastic to protect the environment. The reserve pit is used to get rid of rock cuttings and drilling mud during the process. Finally, several holes are dug for the rig, and then a large, rectangular pit, called a *cellar* is dug where the actual drilling hole will be. This gives the workers room to move about when they start to dig the main hole. They start doing this with a smaller drill, and then when they have the hole started, the main rig is brought in.

Recording 23

[E = Examiner, S = Student]
E: Why are you taking IELTS?
S: Generally, er, because the universities need it, and, er, need to achieve, er, a high score of English level.
E: How long have you been studying English?
S: Five years. I studied at high school in China.
E: How would you describe your home country or your home town?
S: My home town is, er, charcoal, charcoal town. The product major is charcoal. And um, it's not really nice town, it's industrial town.
E: What are the best things about life in your country?
S: Um, Chinese food ... dumplings, something like that.
E: What do you usually do at the weekend?
S: I usually do, play ping pong and swimming in China, and go to fitness clubs.
E: What do you hope to do in the future?
S: I want to be a managing director.

Recording 24

OK, the important day in my life that I'm going to talk about happened about four years ago. This was the day my football team got promoted. The team, er, had played well all that season and had reached the finals and my brother and I were, er, were, er, both keen supporters and we both followed the team, er, for about 15 years. It was a very exciting day for, for the team because they'd never been promoted out of the division into a higher division in their history.

My brother and I got into the football ground about lunchtime and waited for the game to start as the crowd built up – there were about 10,000 people there that day. The game swung from side to side, with first of all, our team scoring and then the other team scoring twice, which was why it was fantastic when our team scored two goals in the last five minutes to win the day and gain promotion to the higher division. The noise at the final whistle was amazing and we were all incredibly excited. I don't think I've ever been to a game where there was such a great atmosphere, before or since. We really celebrated that night, but the next morning, I could hardly speak from all of the shouting I'd been doing!

Recording 25

Student 1

I met my friend in China six years ago. My parents and his parents are, um, workmates and he and me are, were, classmates in high school. And, um, he's in England for three years, and so am I. Er, we study together and live together as well. He studies harder than me and he's, er, very generous and he's, er, quite intelligent as well. So he plays a very important place in my life.

Student 2

OK. I have a friend called Jolie. She's Chinese and we met in the first class, the first English class. We were paired up to do an assignment and that's how we became friends. Umm ... I've known her for about five months and it's been fun. We do ... we help each other with assignments and we go for movies and cook together, have dinners and stuff and just have fun talking, laughing and singing. Um ... I think she's played a very important part in my life because she ... she ... I admire her motivation and dedication and I think she's a very intelligent person and very strong-willed and ... something ... a lot of her character I wish I had in my life so that's why I think she's played an important role in my life.

Recording 26

1 A: Do you enjoy playing sports?
  B: Yes, definitely. I particularly enjoy outdoor ones.
2 A: Would you like to go there again?
  B: Possibly. It would depend on who I went with!
3 A: Do you think it will be easy to get a job in IT?
  B: I expect so. It's a growing industry.
4 A: Have you ever been to any other countries in Europe?
  B: Yes, a few. France, Spain and the Czech Republic.
5 A: Would you consider doing the same sort of job again?
  B: I don't think so. It wasn't really for me.
6 A: Would you recommend the holiday to other people?
  B: No, not really. It wasn't very good value for money.

Recording 27

[E = Examiner, S = Student]
1 E: Do you think it's important for young people to spend time with older people?
  S: Yes. I think young people can learn a lot from older people. For instance, older people have plenty of experience and can give advice on all sorts of problems. On the other hand, younger people have loads of energy and curiosity that they can share with the older generation.
2 E: Do you think children should learn financial planning at school or at home?
  S: My family save its money, but many people is spending all the time. The teachers should teach the students to save.
3 E: Can you think of some of the negative effects of text messaging?
  S: Well, I think text messages are quite, how do you say ... not friendly. Because, you send a funny message, and the other person don't know how you feel and they don't think you joking and get upset with you.
4 E: Which is better: living in the countryside or in the city?
  S: Personally, I like living in the countryside. I like the peace and quiet. But then, on the other hand, you don't have the same facilities in the countryside, like transport and shops. So I suppose that it's actually more practical to live in the city.
5 E: To what extent are qualifications important?
  S: Qualifications are important to get a job. For example, I'm a doctor. I couldn't get a job without qualifications.
6 E: How likely is it that computers will be able to replace humans in the workplace?
  S: Computers have already replaced humans in a lot of ways. For example, in car manufacturing, robots do a lot of the finishing and assembly, where, in the past people did the work. But I don't think computers can take the place of people completely because there are certain jobs, such as nursing that really need human contact.

7 E: Would you prefer to watch sport or play it?

S: Actually, I'm not like sport. I not watching it or play it. I play computer game online. My favorite is X Men. I play with my friends every night.

8 E: How do you think global warming will affect transport in the future?

S: One possibility is that it can become more and more expensive to travel and people cannot to go to other countries so often. Another possibility is that we can have new kinds of transport with wind, solar and hydrogen power.

Practice test

Section 1

Recording 28

[CRA = Car Rental Agent, SM = Sarah Middleton]

CRA: Good morning, Swift Car Rentals. Miriam speaking. How can I help you?

SM: Oh, hello, um, good morning. I'd like to rent a car.

CRA: Good. Well, let's see. What kind of car were you thinking of?

SM: Um ..., there are only two of us and a child, but we have quite a lot of luggage.

CRA: We have small, economy vehicles, like the Mini. But they're only two door and the boot's quite small. A medium-sized car, like the Focus has four doors and plenty of space for bags. Would you want a manual or automatic?

SM: Oh, um ... manual, er ... definitely.

CRA: That's fine, and when do you need the car for?

SM: From Friday to Sunday.

CRA: This coming weekend?

SM: Yes, that's right.

CRA: OK. Well, we have a Focus available from Friday. Would that suit you?

SM: Yes, that sounds OK. A Focus. And how much will it cost?

CRA: Well, we have an offer on at the moment. It's a three day rental at £24 a day. So that would be £72 for the weekend.

SM: Oh, that's good. Does it include insurance and unlimited mileage?

CRA: Yes, that's all inclusive. It covers rental, insurance, unlimited mileage and a breakdown service.

SM: Right, fine ... Would there be any extra cost for a child seat?

CRA: No, we don't charge extra for the child seat. It'll be covered by the security deposit.

SM: Oh ... How much is the deposit, then?

CRA: For that rental it would be £500. We don't actually charge it though. We just need your credit card details to cover us in case there's any damage. How many drivers would there be?

SM: Two drivers. Both over 25.

CRA: That's great. Would you like to make the booking, now?

SM: Yes, please. Let's go ahead with it.

CRA: So, could I have your name, please.

SM: Sarah Middleton.

CRA: Sorry, did you say Middleton? How do you spell that?

SM: M-I-double D-L-E-T-O-N

CRA: And your address?

SM: 15 Drysdale Avenue.

CRA: D-R-I?

SM: No, D-R-Y-S-D-A-L-E.

CRA: OK. And that's in?

SM: Queensborough.

CRA: And the post code?

SM: QL5 8HT.

CRA: QL5 8HT?

SM: Yes. That's right.

CRA: And the other driver's name?

SM: That's Michael Middleton.

CRA: Thank you. And do you both have full driving licences?

SM: Yes, we do.

CRA: Fine. So that's a Ford Focus, four door with a child seat from Friday the 13th to Sunday the 15th of July.

SM: Good. So, what time can we collect the car?

CRA: It'll be available from 7.00 in the morning. When would you like to collect it?

SM: Well, we're planning to set off at around 9.00. So we could pick it up at 8.00. Would that be OK?

CRA: Yes, no problem. That'll give us time to get the paperwork done. You need to bring both your licences and your credit card. You know where we are, don't you?

SM: Yes, Uxwater Road. Is that right?

CRA: That's it. Number 35, just opposite the railway station.

SM: Right. So we'll be there on Friday morning at about 8 o'clock.

CRA: Oh, just one more thing. Have you got a mobile number, too, in case anything goes wrong?

SM: Of course. It's 0791 357629.

CRA: Sorry, did you say 619?

SM: No, 357629.

CRA: Great. Well, we'll see you on Friday, then.

SM: Yes, see you then.

CRA: Thank you. Goodbye.

SM: Bye now.

Section 2

Recording 29

Good afternoon. It's good to see so many of you here. I hope you're all beginning to find your way round the campus. I know it's all a bit confusing the first week ... there's a lot to take in: lectures, clubs and societies, meeting new friends, settling in to your rooms. But I'm glad you've taken time to come and find out about the Sports Centre. I'm David Trent, Sports Centre manager, and I'm going to give you a run down on the services and facilities we have here and tell you what you need to know about joining.

If you're here, you probably already know how important it is to keep fit and healthy while you're studying. It's easy to spend hours in front of the computer screen in your room and forget to exercise, especially when you have an essay to write or an exam to study for. But the Sports Centre is open from 7.00 in the morning to 9.00 in the evening, every day. So you'll have plenty of time to come in for a workout or a fitness class.

So, what do we offer? Well, I've just mentioned workouts. We have a fully equipped fitness suite with treadmills, cycles, rowing machines, exercise machines and weight-lifting equipment. There's also an entertainment system. In one part of the gym you can listen to music while you exercise, and in the other section we have TV screens. Of course, all our equipment also has headphone connections, so you can listen to your own music if you'd prefer. The gym is staffed all day and in the evening by trained instructors, who can give you advice on how to use the equipment. The gym's very popular and does get a bit full at certain times of the day, but there's lots of equipment and you shouldn't have any trouble finding what you want.

I've also mentioned fitness classes. We have a huge range of classes, from yoga to kickboxing. If you like the idea of dancing to get fit, we have belly dancing ... salsa classes, hip hop, and street dancing. Or if you prefer gentle exercise, we have pilates, yoga and tai chi. If you like a really tough workout we have the Ab Lab for abdominals, and some pretty demanding circuit training. Our instructors are all trained and qualified and they'll make sure you get the best out of the sessions.

So far, I haven't mentioned the actual sports facilities. Apart from the fitness suite, we have two large sports halls and ten squash courts. We use the sports halls for badminton, netball, basketball, five-a-side football and handball, as well as for training and fitness sessions. Outside we have tennis courts and several football pitches.

So that's what we have at the moment ... but we're expanding ... and over the next two years we're building an Olympic® size swimming pool. It should be ready before you graduate, so it's a very exciting development.

Finally, how do you become a member of the Sports Centre and how much does it cost? Well, there are two types of membership: peak and off-peak. Peak members can use the fitness suite at any time of day, but off-peak members have limited access. And how do you join? It's very simple ... enrolment is online. You need your student number and you just fill in the form and pay with your credit card. And how much does it cost? Peak membership is £140 a year and off-peak £114. Not a lot of money, really, when you think of all the benefits of a healthy lifestyle.

Now are there any questions ... ?

Section 3

Recording 30

C: Hi, Andrew. How's your Law essay going?

A: Hi, Chen. How are you doing? My essay? Mm ... I think it's going quite well. I'm writing about the globalization of crime. It's fascinating finding out how crime has become a massive international business over the last twenty-five years.

C: Oh ... that does sound interesting. Is it mostly about drug smuggling, then?

A: Well, no. It's much wider than that. The interesting thing is how increased global trading has opened up borders to commerce but at the same time this has meant that crime has spread internationally, too.

C: Yeah ... I suppose that's logical. What kinds of crime are you writing about, actually?

A: Umm ... all kinds really. These days organized crime has expanded way beyond drugs and money laundering. It has links with terrorism, human trafficking, cybercrime, pirates and the production of imitation goods ...

C: Wow. That's quite a big topic. So how are you going to structure your essay?

A: Well ... . First I'm going to talk about international crime and then explain how it has managed to expand so much.

C: So how has it happened, then?

A: OK, ... umm ... over the years organized crime has become very powerful economically by trading legal products illegally. That means that the products they have been trading are OK but the way they are trading isn't. For example, they might sell arms and weapons to a group that is not legally allowed to buy them, like rebels or terrorists. The product, weapons, is perfectly legal, but the trade itself isn't.

C: I see. So it's quite complicated. But isn't there any straighforward crime, like terrorism and piracy?

A: Oh, yes, of course. Organized groups are behind a lot of international criminal activity.

C: Ah, right ... . And which countries are involved most?

A: That's an interesting question, because the flow of illegal trade is highest into and out of the richest countries. But, on top of that a lot of this trade is genuinely transnational. I mean, in the case of human trafficking ... a victim might be taken from one country by an agent from another country and delivered to a client in a third country.

C: So, it's extremely difficult to investigate.

A: Yes. And it's specially hard to get information about the slave trade because the victims are usually living illegally in a country and they don't want to get arrested themselves. So they don't report the criminals to the police. It's what they call a victimless crime.

C: Mmm ... did you look into any other type of crime?

A: Oh, definitely. I was also interested in the trade in endangered species. You know, animals that are becoming extinct for various reasons.

C: Why did you want to look at that, in particular?

A: Well, I wanted to find out if organized crime has any effect beyond the economy. And I discovered that organized groups are heavily involved in trafficking animals from Africa and South-East Asia and responsible for the widespread poaching and killing of rare animals. So, organized crime is also causing environmental harm.

C: It looks as though you've found a really interesting topic, with a lot to write about. You're probably having difficulty deciding how much detail to include and how to focus your argument.

A: Yes, it's a bit difficult to narrow it down. I thought that once I'd discussed the different types of organized international crime, I'd go on to discuss the problem of how to reduce it.

C: So, what is the solution?

A: Well, it's obviously not at all easy. Some of the best brains in the world are working on solutions. In fact, the problem is so big that the United Nations has funded research into it.

C: And what did they find?

A: Umm ... well, it's a long story, but their message is that all illicit trade responds to a market demand and that it isn't enough to simply catch criminal groups at a regional level. There is a need for international cooperation, not only in policing, but also in government policies and regulations.

C: Sounds like a really good essay, Andrew. Let me know how it goes.

Section 4

Recording 31

Over the last few weeks we've been looking at the ethics of spending public and private money on expensive projects that seem to benefit a very small minority of the population.

We've discussed spending on art and architecture and on the Olympic® Games and other sporting events, like the World Cup. This week, I'm going to talk about space exploration.

Ever since the early days of space exploration there's been a lively debate about whether it's right to spend such large amounts of money on something that only a few people benefit from, when there are so many social problems to solve throughout the world. However, there is little doubt that, over the years, research into space travel has led to advances in … in … ummm … other fields, like national security, communications and health. Because the results of this research are not directly related to the original purpose, they're called spinoffs. So … ah … today, I'm going to have a look at a few of these spinoffs.

OK, so … first let's see what the spinoffs in medicine might be. Early research into the effects of space travel on the human body, gave us a greater understanding of our physiology. But more recently, research teams in the International Space Station have been able to do experiments in cell biology that could lead to improvements in the treatment of diabetes and heart disease. And another interesting advance in medicine has been the development of long-distance ultrasound technology, which allows doctors to diagnose patients in isolated places over the internet. And in the field of public health … another development is … umm … water purification systems that can improve the lives and health of millions of people.

Next I'm going to talk about the development of more commercial products, like memory foam, optics and camera technology and insulation. It's not very difficult to see how these products came about as the result of research into space travel. For example, memory foam, which is a special type of plastic that adapts to the shape of a person's body, was developed in order to make the seats in space craft more comfortable. Nowadays it's a popular material for mattresses and pillows. Another example from our daily lives is how the images on our mobile phones and webcams have improved over the years. To a certain extent digital camera technology has advanced because it's so important to receive clear images from space. And, of course, the link between space travel and insulation are fairly obvious. Space craft are subjected to extreme cold once they leave the atmosphere and extreme heat when they return to earth. And this particular field of space research has led to better home insulation and, more vitally, to improvements in fire resistant materials for firefighters. And a quite surprising spinoff from research into preventing damage to space craft has been the development of advanced techniques in art restoration. Then, one more useful invention is a programmable oven that can be controlled from the web. Imagine sending a message from your mobile phone to your oven and having your dinner ready when you get home!

Ahh … to go on … I'd just like to briefly mention a couple of spinoffs in the field of public safety. One is that we can predict local weather conditions more accurately. This can be crucial for planning rescue services in disaster areas or predicting drought or taking action to avoid famine. On top of that, space research has improved air traffic control systems and made flying safer for all of us.

OK … So there you have a number of examples of how space research has benefited society as a whole. But we can still ask whether these benefits are great enough to justify the vast amounts of money spent on the programme. There are many people who feel that the cost of space exploration far outweighs the social benefit. They would argue that with the billions of dollars that are currently channelled into space research we could eliminate famine and disease worldwide. And there are … umm … even more arguments … for example, some people would say that we haven't fully explored our own planet yet, or solved the urgent problem of global warming. They would say that saving our environment should have a higher priority than going off into space.

However, there are arguments against these … umm … I mean, if we spent billions of dollars on eradicating disease and starvation now, how long would that last? Would we be solving the real problem? Because the real problem may lie in the political structures of the developed and developing countries. So, you can see, it's not a simple black and white argument …